F.V.

THE HORRORS OF SLAVERY

The Horrors of Slavery
and Other Writings
by Robert Wedderburn

Edited and introduced by
IAIN McCALMAN

 MARKUS WIENER PUBLISHING
NEW YORK & PRINCETON

© Iain McCalman, 1991

Markus Wiener Publishing Inc.
114 Jefferson Road, Princeton,
NJ 08540

Typeset in Linotron Stempel
Garamond
by Nene Phototypesetters
Ltd, and
printed in Great Britain by
Robert Hartnoll Ltd, Bodmin

Library of Congress Cataloguing
    in Publication Data
Wedderburn, R. (Robert)
    Horrors of slavery and
    other writings / by Robert
    Wedderburn; edited and
    introduced by Iain
    McCalman.
            p.   cm.
    ISBN 1–55876–050–4;
    $34.95. —
    ISBN 1–55876–051–2
    (pbk.); $14.95
    1. Slavery—West Indies—
    History—19th century.
    2. Wedderburn, R. (Robert)
    3. Abolitionists—England
    —London—Biography.
    I. McCalman, Iain.
    II. Title.
    HT1071.W43   1992
    306.3'62'0872909034—dc20
    91–33231
        CIP

ISBN 1–55876–050–4
     1–55876–051–2 (pbk)

Contents

Illustrations

Preface and Acknowledgements

By their nature, the writings in this selection are characterised by numerous misspellings, examples of eccentric grammar, errors of syntax, and the like. These 'mistakes' have been faithfully reproduced and the extracts published in their original form because a major aim of this book is to represent the extraordinary achievement of a man who was poor, unlettered and rough in every sense of the word. It is my hope that, rather than hindering the reader's understanding, this stylistic 'roughness' will actually aid a proper appreciation of Robert Wedderburn and his writings.

I would like to thank the staff and trustees of the British Library and the Public Record Office for allowing me to reproduce manuscript, printed and illustrative materials from their collections. Professor Paul Edwards of the University of Edinburgh and Dr James Walvin of the University of York have kindly supplied me with essential documents and references. Marian Robson, Maree Beer and Helen Boxall from the History Department of the Australian National University have typed and proof-read the manuscript with great skill and patience. My wife Heather has encouraged and helped me throughout.

Abbreviations

Add. MS	British Library Additional Manuscript
HO	Home Office
LCS	London Corresponding Society
PRO	Public Record Office
TS	Treasury Solicitor's Papers

Introduction

Early in 1824 a small pamphlet carrying the melodramatic title of *The Horrors of Slavery* appeared in the Holborn and Smithfield bookshops of several leading London ultra-radicals. Its lengthy subtitle explained that this was the exemplary autobiography of a mulatto Jamaican slave offspring named Robert Wedderburn who had recently been a prisoner in Dorchester gaol 'for conscience-sake'. It did not say that the author was also a ragged Soho tailor and a notorious revolutionary conspirator whose recent imprisonment on a blasphemous libel charge had saved him from certain execution for the more serious crime of high treason.

The publication of this abolitionist autobiography, which marked something of a departure from his previous radical propaganda and activism, probably owed its inspiration to a stranger who had visited his thirty foot by six foot cell in Dorchester's 'Ward of Solitude' two years earlier. Wedderburn had been stunned to discover that his visitor was none other than the famous evangelical abolitionist William Wilberforce himself.[1] We may guess that the 'advice' that Wilberforce offered, along with a gift of two leather-bound books, was for the black to devote himself to the urgent cause of emancipating his West Indian brethren instead of squandering his talents on blaspheming God and subverting the King. The ardent dedication of the subsequent autobiography to Wilberforce, along with an offer to help the abolitionist campaign in parliament, shows that Wedderburn accepted the first part of the advice, but his defiantly radical opening paragraph (Document 1) hints that he rejected the second.

Wedderburn had in fact been convinced for at least a decade that the liberation of West Indian slaves and English working people were inseparable causes. Sadly however, when he returned from Dorchester to London after serving his two year prison sentence, he found the popular radical movement disabled by government repression. On the other hand the abolitionist movement showed signs of revival; even the racy sporting weekly *Bell's Life in London* carried articles strongly hostile to the slaving interest. Inspired by one such report in February 1824[2], Wedderburn submitted to the paper the first of two letters attacking his father, James Wedderburn of Inveresk, who had formerly been a substantial sugar plantation owner and slaveholder in Jamaica. This correspondence, which includes an attempted refutation by one of James Wedderburn's well-to-do sons, Andrew Colvile, as well as an accompanying *Bell's* editorial, makes up the bulk of *Horrors of Slavery*.

The editor of *Bell's* found Robert Wedderburn's story convincing and believed that the mulatto had got the better of the exchange with his merchant half-brother Andrew Colvile (alias Wedderburn). Most modern readers will agree. Moreover, a superb recent account of Jamaican slavery based on the diaries of a slaveholder Thomas Thistlewood, 1750–86, corroborates Wedderburn's general picture of the slave experience and authenticates some specific details of the autobiography. Although Thistlewood makes no mention of Wedderburn's remarkable slave grandmother, Talkee Amy, he cites many examples of slaves operating semi-autonomous businesses selling, or 'higglering', goods for their masters, and he also furnishes details of obeah funeral rituals similar to those she is said to have conducted. His account shows that it was not unusual for slave women to display the rebellious disposition which Wedderburn attributes to his mother, Rosanna, and to incur floggings for such misdemeanors as visiting relatives without permission.

Thistlewood's diaries record several instances of the illegitimate, dislocated and virtually parentless upbringing which so wounded young Robert Wedderburn. And, above all, Thistlewood's precise, unemotional record of his frequent fornications confirms Wedderburn's claims about the sexually predatory character of many Jamaican slaveholders. Supporting evidence of the generality of this trend comes from no less an authority than Wedderburn's own father, Dr James Wedderburn, who told his friend and neighbour Thistlewood 'that of those who have long been on this island … 4/5ths die of the venereal disease, one way or other, occasioned by it'. The diaries further confirm Robert's claims in *Horrors of Slavery* that his father practised as a doctor and male midwife 'drugging and physicing poor blacks' and that he also ran an estate where he purchased, hired and sold slaves.[3]

At one level, Robert Wedderburn's *Horrors of Slavery* can be seen as a contribution to the genre of abolitionist autobiography pioneered by three distinguished late eighteenth-century black Londoners, Ignatius Sancho, Ottobah Cugoano and Olaudah Equiano.[4] True, there is no evidence that Wedderburn knew any of their writings, though it is possible that a black autobiography was among the prison gifts from which the imprisoned mulatto 'derived much ghostly consolation' (1: 72). Naturally the provenance and emphasis of Wedderburn's tract also reflects a later phase of the abolitionist struggle when important battles had been won and the movement was taking a more democratic shape.[5] And, unlike his predecessors, Wedderburn could not testify directly to the experience of having been a slave: he had not been born in Africa[6], had not undergone the horrors of the middle passage and had not felt the monstrous indignity of being treated as a human commodity. Even so, he shares enough affinities to belong within the same broad tradition.

Wedderburn was after all a direct product, witness and victim of the Jamaican slave system. It was the crucible of his being, as every one of his writings and speeches in some way reveals. Its effects haunted him until death. His autobiography shows just how difficult it was for a young Kingston mulatto, however nominally free, to escape the warp of institutional slavery. Whether or not deliberately, *Horrors of Slavery* thus echoes many of the themes of slave autobiographies. Separation from his slave mother in infancy and his white father's denial of paternity taught him as surely as it did Sancho, Cugoano and Equiano what it was like to grow up without parents. He recounts, too, a familiar but harrowing story of what it was like as a small child to watch his mother and grandmother being flogged and sexually exploited, and of the slave owner's repeated indifference to all bonds of family feeling. And he presents compelling examples of slave resilience and resistance through the rebellious violence of his African-born mother, Rosanna, and the resourceful sagacity of his grandmother, Amy.

In many ways Wedderburn's subsequent experiences as an immigrant in Britain also resembled those of several of his black abolitionist predecessors. He, like Equiano, joined the British navy, saw action at sea and landed in England for the first time in late boyhood. Like Cugoano and Equiano, he became a poor working man who lived and worked on the fringes of the ragged community of fellow 'blackbirds' in London. He, too, underwent an evangelical conversion which left its mark in his use of biblical imagery, language and textual reference. He shared the same intense pre-occupation with the question of his identity as a 'man of colour' or 'African', and the same sense of kinship with the black slave society from which he sprang. He, too, depended heavily on white patrons for literary, financial and technical help in producing his auto-biography. And, like Equiano, he eventually joined the English popular radical movement which had emerged in response to the detonations of the American and French revolutions.

Yet these resemblances can also be misleading; closer scrutiny shows that Wedderburn's life and writings differed from those of all of his black abolitionist predecessors in crucial ways, and it is precisely these differences which make him such a unique witness of the black plebeian experience in Britain. The dominant theme in the autobiographical works of Sancho, Cugoano and Equiano is self improvement; each represents his life and writing as evidence of the ability of blacks to better themselves educationally and morally in the face of great personal disadvantage.[7] Wedderburn presents himself rather as a social failure and victim who explains his 'misconduct' and 'misfortunes' by his 'unfortunate origins' as a slave offspring (1). Respectable and influential patronage never came his way. The closest he came to receiving help from his wealthy Scottish family was a cracked sixpence and some small beer dispensed by a kindly servant at a time when the mulatto and his pregnant wife were close to starvation. Education also eluded him: such teaching as he was given as a child stopped around the age of four; unlike Equiano or Sancho, he remained of limited literacy in English, though like Equiano, his talent for public speaking was notable.

Above all, Wedderburn was never befriended or aided by influential white abolitionists as were his three predecessors. His only known contact of this sort seems to have been Wilberforce's prison visit of 1822, and even this may have had mixed motives given the famous evangelical's penchant for trying to convert imprisoned working-class free-thinkers.[8] The sort of patrons that Wedderburn did attract were hardly likely to increase his respectability. George Cannon, who secretly revised or ghosted much of the black's published work in 1819–21, was a down-at-heel solicitor, preacher and free-thinker, as well as a fringe revolutionary and putative pornographer. And William Dugdale, Wedderburn's friend and follower who provided the publishing and printing facilities for *Horrors of Slavery*, had similarly turned from revolutionary plotting to pornographic publishing.[9] Even the newspaper which published Wedderburn's original autobiographical letters specialised in sensationalism and circulated extensively 'among the very lowest part of the population.'[10]

It is this unrespectability or roughness which distinguishes Wedderburn so decisively from his predecessors. And thanks to the many spies, informers and undercover policemen who tried to keep him under surveillance, we are afforded a rare glimpse of his political and social underworld—the world of someone who might otherwise have disappeared into obscurity amongst those whom James Walvin has called 'the subterranean mass of rootless poor blacks'.[11] Because of the survival of these government records, *Horrors of Slavery* is not the only, nor the most important, source of Wedderburn's life, language and ideas. Needless to say intelligence reports have to be treated with extreme caution, and the examples included in this book are offered in that spirit. They represent a small sample from a collection which encompasses the activities of mutually-unsuspecting spies, informers, policemen, specialist shorthand writers and nosy passers-by, as well as the testimonies of frightened, hostile or sympathetic neighbours, friends and relatives. Through them we can catch an echo from a black underground—the pungent colloquialisms and West Indian inflections of Robert Wedderburn's voice.

Indeed, it is as a speaker rather than a writer in the conventional sense that we should try to approach this rough and unlettered man. In his own day his influence derived less from published tracts than from the power of his personality projected through gesture and speech—as a tavern orator, debater and singer, as well as a radical preacher and performer. Sensitivity to these non-literary dimensions helps us to reconstruct the mentality and creative energies of someone from this most marginal and supposedly inarticulate of backgrounds. We may also begin to appreciate how significant was the achievement of a penniless and uneducated black who became so notorious that the Prince Regent himself feared his revolutionary activities. Such political extremism represents a further dividing line between Wedderburn and earlier black abolitionists. Because he lived long enough to experience the more class-conscious and polarised popular radicalism of the early nineteenth century, he developed a set of revolutionary political ideas and practices that would have been inconceivable to his pioneering predecessors.

I

Readers who know something of Olaudah Equiano's life may think that Wedderburn's distinctiveness has been overstated. A former slave, royal naval seaman, evangelical enthusiast, black immigrant and member of the Jacobinical London Corresponding Society, Equiano would seem to have anticipated the patterns of Robert Wedderburn's life in numerous ways. Here again, though, the crucial dividing line is respectability. As a free mulatto child in Kingston under the charge of the slave obeah and smuggler's agent, 'Talkee' Amy, Wedderburn grew up outside the boundaries of legal, social and religious orthodoxy.

Like Equiano before him he then escaped the worst of slave society by service in the British navy, yet he responded to the experience differently. Equiano used seafaring life as a way of demonstrating superior educational ambition and moral practice, the latter significantly rooted by him in his Ibo origins; often Equiano draws attention to the indiscipline, profanity and brutality of the rabble below decks.[12] Wedderburn also saw action against the French aboard a British man o'war, but he complained rather of the surfeit of discipline in the navy. The savage flogging of sailors in wartime recalled the world of slavery, and he echoed the grievances of those common sailors—blacks amongst them—who mutinied so dramatically at the Nore and Spithead in 1797.[13] And in his case shipboard life evidently did nothing to enhance respectability; years later spies were still likening his rough, salty language to that of a sailor, one of the reasons, perhaps, why he numbered seamen amongst his most ardent admirers in 1819–20.[14]

Interestingly, the seventeen year old Robert Wedderburn disembarked in England around 1778, close to the time that thirty-two year old Olaudah Equiano landed on English soil for the third and last time. Here again the experiences of immigration pressed differently on the two men. Without minimising the hardships and racial slights that Equiano encountered in London, he was able to extract some consolation from the friendship and admiration of many upper-class white abolitionists. The more usual fate of discharged black and lascar sailors, claimed one Home Office correspondent in 1814, was to end up in 'the madhouse, poorhouse or Bridewell'. In the decades that followed, Wedderburn had his taste of the last two institutions at least. He gravitated to the vicinity of the St Giles 'rookeries' where a community of fellow 'blackbirds' scraped a living as musicians, actors, street entertainers, prize fighters, casual labourers, and thieves. It was probably here that he formed an association with 'an abandoned set of reprobates' which over the early years brought him at least one spell in Coldbath Fields prison and a near miss on a charge of theft as late as 1813.[15]

Although the poverty and conspicuousness of blacks encouraged predatory crimping gangs, blood money informers and Bow Street runners, Wedderburn seems not to have met with much racial discrimination within this poor immigrant underworld. By contrast, another Jamaican mulatto immigrant, William 'Black' Davidson, who moved initially in middle-class circles, complained of receiving bitter and wounding treatment as 'a stranger in a strange land', until he too was reduced to the status of an unemployed artisan and pauper.[16] The poverty, even criminality, of these blacks did not necessarily reflect a lumpen mentality however. Men and women from this milieu could express their disaffection through the time-honoured tradition of riot, and we know that the violent behaviour of the eighteenth-century London crowd was often underpinned by a more than rudimentary political consciousness. Sancho and Wedderburn responded to the ferocious Gordon riots of June 1780 in significantly different ways: Sancho berated the rioters from behind his battened-down shop[17]; Wedderburn looked on approvingly and later boasted of his friendship with one of the ringleaders. He may even have participated in the destruction and looting without being caught, unlike a fellow black who was executed for her part in the affair. One suspects that Wedderburn was lucky during these years to escape the fate of many of his black countrymen who had to endure a replication of slave conditions as convict transportees to Van Dieman's Land or Botany Bay.[18]

The truculent libertarianism which Wedderburn was to flaunt in later speeches could equally have been acquired whilst working in London as a journeyman tailor. He does not tell us how or when he learned this trade—whether in Jamaica like his millwright half-brother, James, or at sea, or in London itself. Gaining admission to such a proud old handicraft trade could not at any rate have been easy, especially given the history of City ordinances designed to prevent blacks from entering trade apprenticeships.[19] Moreover Wedderburn claimed the title of 'flint' tailer, indicating that he belonged to the fraternity of 'exclusives' or 'honourables' whose names were registered in the book of trades. As such he shared the typical values of the late-eighteenth century London artisan: pride in craft and status; a fierce belief in rights to economic independence, a living wage and social respect; and a profound contempt for unskilled 'dung' tailors who accepted sweated conditions and wages. At the same time the former London tailor and labour archivist Francis Place assures us that artisan pride did not in the late eighteenth century carry its later connotations of moral respectability. Place's autobiography describes a pervasive 'blackguard' culture shared by lowly apprentice and master journeymen alike, and characterised by workshop pilfering, promiscuous sexuality and drunken conviviality.[20] This was Wedderburn's world.

In trades like tailoring and shoemaking the status of honourable artisan also offered no insulation against steadily declining wages and conditions due to changes in the labour process such as the systematic exploitation of unskilled labour. Though artisans might hope to maintain themselves and their families independently without resorting to charity, crime or profligacy, success was usually dependent upon luck, or some access to patronage, capital and educational resources. Without these, failure at some point in the life cycle was almost certain, especially as competition within the London handicraft trades intensified during the Napoleonic Wars.[21] Wedderburn seems to have been one of the many casualties. By the postwar years he was reported to be scraping a bare living as a 'jobbing tailor', patching clothes and vending pamphlets from a wooden stall located within one of the tiny stinking courts off St Martin's Lane. The disjunction between his pride as an artisan and his degradation as a ragged piece-worker, beggar and thief probably goes a long way towards explaining why he eventually became a radical.

II

Some working men in Wedderburn's desperate position found consolation and a measure of respectability through evangelical religion, especially in its burgeoning Methodist form. Evangelical conversion featured prominently in the lives of all of Wedderburn's black literary predecessors and it has been rightly interpreted as an important source of their social acceptance and cultural integration.[22] Wedderburn's conversion took place around 1786 in the heartland of London's poor black community, Seven Dials, when he overheard a Wesleyan preacher haranguing a crowd. His description of the process appears in a small theological treatise, *Truth Self Supported*, published around 1802, and represented here (2), though much of it is—in the words of one nineteenth-century reader—'unintelligible to common understandings'. Nevertheless it is in some respects an orthodox example of working-class spiritual autobiography, a genre which goes back at least as far as Bunyan. *Truth Self Supported* describes Wedderburn's formerly profligate life, his agonising realisation of guilt and sin, and his surge of elation at receiving the gift of grace. Cugoano and Equiano recorded similar experiences, as did scores of other humble Englishmen.

One modern historian has described such Methodistic works as 'Custard Piety',[23] but custard is not the image which the detonation of Wedderburn's conversion tends to evoke. Moreover, there is no evidence in his case that the experience caused any rupture of his West Indian cultural heritage. Wedderburn claims to have been raised as a Christian until around the age of five, and thereafter to have come under the tutelage of his grandmother, the African-born slave obeah 'Talkee Amy'. Throughout his life he continued to believe in the formidable magical powers which she deployed when presiding over funeral rituals, placating offended spirits, and dispensing personal good and bad luck (1: 49–50).[24] She carried something of the flavour, too, of the traditional cunning rogue, trickster or 'ginal' of West Indian-African folklore. When Wedderburn later claimed to have been prone to religious feelings even before he left Jamaica, he was thus referring to a syncretic fusion of obeah and Christian belief. Historians and anthropologists have noted how readily such belief systems could be laced together within social and cultural contexts ranging from North American and West Indian slave societies to modern West African nativist-Christian cults.[25]

His Methodist conversion in England may actually have nourished this pabulum of magic. Recent authorities have argued that much of early Methodism's popular appeal rested on its ability to echo traditional English folk belief and community practice, reflected in its 'segregation by sex and age within a binding sense of congregation', its acceptance of key elements of popular superstition, its theological imagery of blood, death and fertility, and its stress on the instructional and inspirational role of song.[26] It is unnecessary and perhaps impossible to disentangle the West Indian and English components of Wedderburn's belief; the point is rather that he discovered marked compatibilities between the two religious cultures. In *Horrors of Slavery*, for example, he notes how Talkee Amy's powers of sorcery are reinforced by 'a judgement of God', and it was her influence—he later implied—which explained his enduring fascination with the Witch of Endor and Balaam's Ass incidents in the scriptures. When he linked the textual argument of *Truth Self Supported* to half a dozen appended hymns (2: 73–7), he was testifying to the affective power of Methodist hymnody over people of African, as well as English, descent. Interestingly, the radical American black abolitionist, David Walker, concluded his powerful *Appeal to the Coloured Citizens of the World* of 1830 similarly[27], and even modern black Afro-Baptists are attracted to the rousing hymns of these same eighteenth-century divines.[28]

Because of Methodism's sober reputation historians sometimes assume that conversion led inevitably to political conservatism and social respectability. This can be misleading: Equiano's intense piety has plausibly been seen as a demand for social recognition and respect. Methodism could also carry its converts in other more heterodox directions. William Hamilton Reid, a renegade London Jacobin whose exposé of 1790s popular radicalism anticipated *Truth Self Supported* by a few years, regarded plebeian Methodism as a dangerously combustible force which recruited from the same social milieux as revolutionary Jacobinism and shared its disaffected political outlook. He noted the tendency of working-class converts to become self-confident and then subversive as they graduated from evangelical preaching to independent radical prophecy[29] (the missionary John Shipman commented similarly on Baptist mulatto preachers in Jamaica).[30] Methodism's rather sedate nineteenth-century image belied its often explosive eschatological origins; Wesley was much troubled in early days by the tendency of his preachers to stray into chiliastic prophecy and sometimes antinomianism as well.

In Georgian and Regency England 'millennialism' was also a highly regarded and widely practised form of scholarly analysis. Plebeian prophets or 'millenarians', however, usually aspired to turn the world upside down in the dangerous fashion of 'Cromwell's preachers'. Seemingly providential threats to Catholic monarchy and Papacy during the troubled 1790s unleashed a torrent of this type of millenarian speculation in London. For all his individual genius William Blake was a more typical figure in his day than many scholars have realised. Wedderburn knew nothing of him, but he declared himself impressed by the prophetic example of a fellow naval veteran, abolitionist and Soho neighbour named Richard Brothers. 'The Prince of Hebrews', as Brothers styled himself, attracted a considerable following by preaching a brand of subversive social prophecy which overlapped with and resembled political Jacobinism.

Significantly, *Truth Self Supported* was published and sold by one of Brothers' most ardent disciples, though there is no evidence that Wedderburn met Brothers personally before 1795 when the fiery prophet was silenced by incarceration in Bedlam. Even if they did not meet, Methodism could itself provide a slipway to prophecy, as in the case of the famous Plymouth prophetess, Joanna Southcott, and the early nineteenth-century radical prophet, John 'Zion' Ward. The parallels between Ward and his two West Indian contemporaries, Wedderburn and Davidson, are particularly striking: all were ex-sailors, immigrants to London from a foreign country, degraded handicraftsmen and former Methodist converts.[31] Even the millenarian currents which Ward encountered in his country of origin, Ireland, had their Jamaican counterparts in the magical world of obeah and the prophetic speculations of free mulatto Baptist preachers in Kingston.

Truth Self Supported may strike some modern readers as merely muddled rather than seditious, and there is no doubt that it represents an early phase in Wedderburn's progression to religious and political heterodoxy. Nevertheless, a close reading discloses some of the potentially subversive elements which so troubled commentators like Reid and Shipman. Wedderburn boasts of the superiority of his powers of exegesis; he scorns the timidity of Established and Dissenting preachers; he is proud of having graduated through various denominations and sects; he displays an almost antinomian conviction of having been freed from sin through grace; he rejects the pivotal doctrine of the Trinity and he deploys an ominous millenarian hint of God's coming wrath (2).

All these signs would have been interpreted by contemporary loyalists as the first fledgling steps of a millenarian prophet. This is

not to say that Wedderburn was a 'madman enthusiast' like his
London contemporaries James Hadlee, Bannister Trulock or John
Bellingham: all notorious plebeian prophets who made assassination attempts on the King or Prime Minister during this period.
Rather, he had begun to blend scriptural millenarianism and
political anticlericalism in ways that resembled seventeenth-century
prophetic radicalism, as well as the more current French revolutionary utopianism. To borrow an analogy from the history of North
American slave revolt, Wedderburn's cast of mind was less that of
the driven visionary, Nat Turner, then the syncretic and pragmatic
millenarian, Denmark Vesey.[32]

All this helps to explain the puzzle as to why Robert Wedderburn, a man without any previous known radical connections,
should suddenly have involved himself in revolutionary politics at a
time of political repression and popular apathy. His retrospective
letter (3) indicates that he joined Thomas Spence's circle of ex-
Jacobin revolutionaries and agrarian radicals in 1813, at the peak of
Napoleon's unpopularity in England. True, Spence had been virtually alone in keeping alive a small revolutionary Jacobin underground during the war years, and his organisation was probably
benefiting from a slight resurgence in radical publication and
electoral politics after 1810. Many of the fresh recruits during these
early Regency years seem to have been, like Wedderburn, London
artisans who were suffering the effects of wartime inflation and of
competition from unskilled workers. Spence's 'plan' promoted a
revolutionary agrarian utopia in which private land and other
resources would be expropriated and offered up to public rental
through the parishes. The resulting funds would be redistributed for
the benefit of the populace—an idea which appealed to degraded
artisans longing to restore their lost rights to economic independence and social respect. Moreover, having himself been reduced
from schoolmaster to ragged street vendor, Spence was indifferent
to the usual credentials of respectability. His boozy alehouse
free-and-easies gathered up immigrants, petty criminals and other
members of the outcast poor, along with struggling artisans and a
sprinkling of marginal middle-class clerks, surgeons, journalists and
lawyers. His propaganda matched this social diversity, ranging from
literary periodicals and tracts to street ballads, wall chalkings and
metal tokens intended to appeal to the less literate.

Wedderburn's transition to radical politics was probably also triggered by Spence's affinities with millenarianism and prophecy. Spence's boyhood in Newcastle had exposed him to currents of popular piety, radical Presbyterianism and folkmagic, though his most recent biographer believes that it was the disorienting experience of moving to London, combined with millenarian movements there, that pushed him into adopting an eschatological language and vision. Having been steeped in enlightenment thought as well, Spence expected his agrarian utopia to come about through an earthly, rationalist revolution of the social and economic order. He always believed that the age of reason and the millennium would proceed hand in hand, but the scriptures gave him his favourite model of social transformation in the Levitical Jubilee of Moses. The language, mores and structure of communitarian Christianity thus informed almost everything he wrote.[33] Former Methodists like Wedderburn and Black Davidson seem to have been attracted to Spenceanism initially as an extension of their earlier links with popular evangelical religion. When Wedderburn joined the Spencean circle in 1813 he was already a licensed dissenting minister. In the opening numbers of a small weekly periodical which he edited and wrote in 1817 he casts himself as a Spencean prophet or enthusiast who has undergone an ecstatic conversion to the movement's ideals and goals (4).

The title of Wedderburn's periodical, *Axe Laid to the Root* echoes Paine, Spence and the Bible, but the subtitle, *Being An Address to the Planters and Negroes of the Island of Jamaica*, hints that he was attracted to Spenceanism for West Indian as much as English reasons. It is important to realise that abolitionist and liberal enlightenment ideas of the kind introduced to London Jacobins by Equiano in the 1790s had been largely crushed during Pitt's suppression of the democratic political societies. Here, as is in many other instances, Spence's circle constituted an important exception.

Alone of the surviving popular radicals, Spence kept a residue of these ideas alive in his shadowy tavern underground during the Napoleonic wars. He published several tracts during these years using American Indian and African communities as models for his proposed Spencean utopia. His writings, songs and speeches also invoked the example of the biblical liberation of the chosen people from Egyptian slavery, an inspirational metaphor which men like Wedderburn and Davidson would probably have earlier heard from the mouths of free mulatto preachers in Kingston. Spence used this and other texts to draw abolitionist conclusions and to make comparisons between plantation slavery in the New World and English landed monopoly in the old. William Cowper's poignant 'Negro's Lament' which Wedderburn reproduced in *Axe Laid to the Root*, along with other popular abolitionist poems and ballads, appeared first in Spence's own periodical of 1814, *Giantkiller*.[34] Spence's apocalyptic promise of land redistribution may also have reawakened that characteristic longing to own and cultivate a small plot which was so frequently expressed by West Indian blacks—slave and free alike.[35] And perhaps Spencean tavern fraternities and communitarian ideals satisfied deep personal needs in Wedderburn, serving as a surrogate for the family he had lost in childhood.

Whatever the diverse sources of its attraction, Spenceanism appears to have provided the ragged mulatto preacher with an exhilarating new cosmology, political critique and social prescription. Now for the first time he was able to make sense of his shaping experiences as a West Indian slave offspring, degraded London artisan and popular evangelical prophet.

III

Wedderburn was not of course the first black to forge links between abolitionism and the English popular radical movement; Olaudah Equiano had in the 1790s befriended the founder of the London Corresponding Society, Thomas Hardy, and joined his democratic organisation.[36] But Equiano died too soon to develop this association—indeed, the year of his death, 1797, marks a watershed in the history of London popular radicalism. In the summer of that year a small group of LCS officeholders, goaded by the Pitt government's crushing of the democratic political societies, decided to abandon constitutionalist moderation in favour of armed revolution. Led by a braces maker, Thomas Evans, this revolutionary fraction formed the United Englishmen, an armed underground society committed to bringing about a republican revolution on the English mainland in conjunction with a French invasion and a United Irish uprising in Ireland. However, the efficiency of the government's intelligence network exposed the society to swift government repression: by the end of 1803 most of the British and Irish revolutionary leaders had been imprisoned, exiled, transported or executed. The Metropolitan remnants—including Evans himself

—attached themselves to Thomas Spence's informal 'underground' of free-and-easy singing and debating clubs held in rough alehouses like 'The Fleece' in Windmill Street and 'The Swan' in New Street.[37] Wedderburn probably first encountered them at the latter which was just around the corner from his tailoring stall.

Even so, joining the group can have been no casual undertaking: by becoming a member of the Jacobin revolutionary underground Wedderburn was—at the age of fifty—beginning a serious flirtation with treason. And although the mood of the veteran plotters tended to be cautious during these years, they were at the time of his recruitment trying to promote a French invasion through the agency of emigré Jacobins in Paris. One of the leading figures in these plans was an ex-militia officer and small-time landowner from Lincolnshire known as 'Captain' Arthur Thistlewood. Unbeknown to Wedderburn, this fellow Spencean recruit was the nephew of Thomas Thistlewood, the slave-owning friend and neighbour of his own father James Wedderburn.[38] Arthur Thistlewood's decline from a relatively genteel background seems to have exacerbated his militancy. After Spence died in October 1814 and was succeeded by Thomas Evans, Thistlewood and another new member, James Watson, pushed the Spenceans to adopt more confronting tactics.

By the postwar winter of 1816 when trade recession, high bread prices and demobilisation were beginning to generate mass unrest in the streets of London, Evans could no longer contain his more headstrong companions. Thistlewood, Watson and a shoemaker, Thomas Preston, broke from the Spenceans to promote a national radical association under the leadership of a charismatic Bristol merchant, Henry 'Orator' Hunt. Outwardly these former Spenceans espoused the 'constitutionalist' tactics of the mass platform—countrywide simultaneous meetings designed to intimidate the government into conceding parliamentary reform or to serve as a springboard for an armed uprising. At the same time they secretly planned an armed *coup d'état*. Its slim chances of success were spoiled on 2 December 1816 when Watson's wild and alcoholic younger son seized a tricolour after a mass meeting at Spa Fields in London and then led a crowd in an attack on a gunshop, followed by an abortive attempt on the Tower.[39] One of the cutlass-wielding ringleaders captured on the day proved to be a black American sailor named Richard Simmonds. He claimed under interrogation that several other blacks and mulattos had been involved in the rising.[40] Wedderburn may have been one of these: his friend and patron, George Cannon, seems to have provided the legal advice which enabled Simmonds to escape with a relatively light sentence of transportation, unlike an Irish fellow sailor named Cashman who was executed for joining the mob.

Whether or not Wedderburn had been implicated in the rising, there is no doubt that for the next few years he remained determinedly loyal to Thomas Evans's leadership, tactics and programme. Evans was not averse to armed revolution, as his prison record in the 1790s showed, but he was deeply committed to Spence's agrarian plan and also feared that premature confrontations would play into the hands of a ruthlessly repressive government. He preferred to mask his revolutionary intentions behind a series of outwardly legal, though highly flexible, tavern debating clubs.[41] Even this did not save him from being arrested on suspicion of high treason during a concerted government crackdown on radical societies in January 1817; he was held in prison for twelve months under the Suspension of Habeas Corpus. In his absence Robert Wedderburn became the unofficial leader of the Spenceans. Spies began to report his 'inflammatory' speeches, noting that he was coordinating the half-dozen debating club 'sections' located in the centre and East End of the metropolis. Later in the year when fear of government reprisal caused these to shrink to a tiny residue at the Mulberry Tree tavern in Moorfields, Wedderburn rallied their spirits with his blasphemous-radical oratory and his small, combative periodicals, *Forlorn Hope* and *Axe Laid to the Root*.

Substantial extracts from the latter are reproduced here in Part III. Though addressed to the planters and slaves of Jamaica, the realistic target of the periodical had to be English wage slaves, particularly those ragged artisans who were buying it in low Spencean alehouses or from Wedderburn's tailoring stall near St Martins Lane. In some respects its contents reflected Wedderburn's immediate political predicament during the winter of 1817. As *de facto* leader of the Spenceans he was faced with fights on several fronts: he had to prevent his members from dropping out of politics or from deserting to rival radical groupings, without at the same time falling into the clutches of a government whose parliamentary Secret Committee of 1817 had branded the Spenceans as a dangerously treasonous organization. The periodical's Jamaican slave context thus provided an analogue of political repression within which he could urge Spencean revolutionary goals and tactics without imperilling himself or the Society.

This dangerous political context helps to explain the relatively moderate blueprint for slave liberation contained in the opening pages of *Axe Laid to the Root* (4). The recommended goals and tactics are those he wishes the London Spenceans to adopt in the repressive climate of autumn and winter 1817. He urges his nominal slave readers to eschew both armed uprisings and meetings to petition the King. True to Spencean principles, he criticises the standard radical goal of parliamentary reform as a half-measure which fails to address the fundamental source of oppression—aristocratic monopoly of private land. Instead, he urges the continued diffusion of Spencean propaganda, combined with a symbolic work stoppage for an hour at a specified signal. This last tactic—a variant of which was actually used by slaves during the Demerara revolt of 1823—represents Wedderburn's adaptation of the artisanal 'national holiday', a political withdrawal of labour which had been suggested to the London Spenceans in January 1817 by a radical delegate from Manchester named William Benbow.[42]

In the last article of this first number of *Axe Laid to the Root* (4) Wedderburn suddenly strikes a new, more apocalyptic note—not relinquishing diffusionist methods, but for the first time embracing armed violence as well. He invokes both the famous St Domingo revolutionary uprising and the Maroon Wars in which communities of runaway slaves conducted successful guerilla campaigns against the British in the mountainous jungle hinterland of Jamaica. This newfound militancy might have come from Wedderburn's growing confidence in his success as a Spencean leader or from a feeling of desperation as legislative and judicial repression began to choke off remaining outlets of popular protest and opinion. Either way, there is no doubting his pugnacity and courage, which is well captured in a contemporary print by George Cruikshank. It depicts the ragged mulatto preacher with raised fist and bible in pocket confronting Robert Owen and other reformers at the famous City of London Tavern meeting of August 1817 (see Fig. 2).

Like other plebeian radicals of his day Wedderburn suspected that Owen's cooperative plan was a political diversion generated by a member of the wealthy and respectable ruling class. In its place, numbers 2–4 of his periodical (4, 5) outline the Spencean-based utopia which Jamaican slaves (and implicitly his London readers) should implement in the aftermath of a successful revolt. Borrowing his inspiration from Spence's own 'Crusoenian' utopia (itself inspired by Harrington and Swift), Wedderburn here presents his most detailed manifesto for a democratic republic of agrarian smallholders to replace both the existing slave system and the corrupt English government and society. At the same time he warns his readers against the false and facile remedies prescribed by rival radical leaders such as Watson, Owen or the moderate Westminster reformer, Sir Francis Burdett.

Even regarded solely within its English context, *Axe Laid to the Root* is a remarkable publication. True, Wedderburn's breathless, hortatory style, erratic punctuation and vernacular language do not make for easy comprehension. To appreciate the periodical's novelty and power we need to treat it as a series of oral sermons designed to be read out to semi-literate audiences in alehouses and workshops. Its impact must also have been enhanced by Wedderburn's skilful incorporation of other familiar plebeian modes such as melodramatic balladry, Bunyanesque dream visions and humorous burlesque. Yet Wedderburn himself rightly believed that the periodical's most important contribution to popular radical ideology came from its sustained attempt to integrate the prospect of slave revolution in the West Indies with that of working-class revolution in England. It thereby extended the pioneering ideas of Equiano and enriched London popular radicalism's standard anti-establishment critique which at that time still owed most of its categories to Cobbett's denunciations of 'Old Corruption'.

Axe Laid to the Root is also notable as a plebeian contribution to the abolitionist cause and a rousing tocsin of West Indian slave revolution in its own right. Much of its power derives from Wedderburn's ability to create the impression that he really is addressing a black West Indian audience. He sustains this illusion by including snippets of gossip supposedly overheard by a slave relative (4), or reprints of letters from his slaveowning half-sister, Miss Campbell, which describe her conversations with exultant freed slaves and frightened planters in the Kingston Assembly (6, 7). Here Wedderburn displays something of Cobbett's flair for dramatising politics by placing his cast of characters in vivid, concrete settings. He also takes care to incorporate details of the history and current affairs of the West Indies. He was probably the first English plebeian radical to make substantial use of the St Domingo (Haitian) revolution of the 1790s which was simultaneously inspiring subject blacks across the Atlantic such as Denmark Vesey, leader of the Charleston slave revolt of 1822, and David Walker, author of the powerful abolitionist *Appeal* of 1830.[43]

Wedderburn was surely unique, though, amongst both radicals and contemporary black theorists, in drawing extensively on the history of the Maroons of St Domingo and Jamaica. Not surprisingly he chose to overlook their ambiguous role as hunters of slave runaways, concentrating instead on their inspirational achievements as guerilla fighters against vastly more powerful Spanish and British forces.[44] They also furnished him with a model of a free black small-holder community to which Spencean theory could be applied. Some of his prescriptions for a post-revolutionary black society seem to have been borrowed from Maroon practices, such as his suggestion that disputes be decided on the spot by village juries composed of men and women elders (5). Miss Campbell, his example of an enlightened Jamaican landowner who supposedly liberates her slaves and reorganises her estate along Spencean principles, is also given a Maroon ancestry: 'I who am a weak woman, of the Maroon tribe understand the Spencean doctrine directly' (7: 107).

Given the rapidity of communication between Jamaica and Britain, there may also have been a grain of truth in Wedderburn's claim that radical ideas were reaching the free mulatto population of Kingston through smuggled copies of *Cobbett's Political Register* and his own *Axe Laid to the Root*. But even if all these Jamaican details were fabricated, they bespeak impressive imaginative power. Wedderburn's evocation of the Jamaican slave setting not only introduced London radicals to new political metaphors and sources of inspiration, but also served as a manifesto of black pride. He could not disguise his elation that poor African slaves, supposedly the most wretched and degraded people on earth, had through the St Domingo revolution and the Maroon Wars liberated themselves at a time when the free-born Englishman was becoming increasingly enslaved. He similarly extolled many of the customs and practices of Jamaican blacks as superior to those of supposedly free and democratic Britons (5). And he was convinced that Jamaican slaves were on the brink of throwing off their fetters through violent revolt, thereby offering a further source of inspiration to their oppressed English brethren. Arguably, it is as a spokesman for this black pride and achievement that Wedderburn most resembles his eighteenth-century predecessors, Cugoano and Equiano.

IV

Spies who noted Wedderburn's eruptions of chiliastic fervour in 1817 predicted that he would not long be satisfied with the cautious tactics of Thomas Evans. Actually, he remained loyal to the Spenceans for a further year. This was partly because of the respect accorded him by Evans after the veteran revolutionary was finally released from prison early in 1818. In recognition of the outstanding success of Wedderburn's religious and political oratory at the Mulberry Tree during the previous winter of 1817, Evans decided to recast the Spencean Society as a Nonconformist sect called the Christian Philanthropists. By using the Haymarket basement in Arthur Street as its licensed chapel and Wedderburn as its preacher, the new Spencean organisation was able to shelter behind the broad oak of religious dissent. Dissenting minister's licences were easy to get, particularly if, like Wedderburn, the applicant described himself as a Unitarian. Wedderburn had been convinced by an anti-Trinitarian sermon in Bristol many years earlier, but he also called himself a Unitarian because William Smith's Trinity Bill of 1813 effectively legalised a broad spectrum of rationalist doctrine. This was one of several advantages that the new Spencean chapel possessed in resisting the state's formidable apparatus of repression. Try as he might, the Home Secretary, Lord Sidmouth, could come up with no viable legal formula for outlawing this radical sect without offending the prickly sensibilities of England's powerful Nonconformist lobby.[45]

Home Office spies took some consolation from signs of a growing rift between the two Spencean leaders caused mainly by Wedderburn's extremism, unrespectability and newfound self confidence. Towards the end of 1818 this tension culminated in a violent quarrel; the two men scuffled in the street after Wedderburn had left the chapel taking the benches and a band of militant Spencean followers with him. In April 1819, amidst swelling popular unrest over poor harvests and a renewed trade slump, Wedderburn opened his own chapel based in a large hayloft in Hopkins Street, Soho. It quickly became a focal point of ultra-radical propaganda and practice. Wedderburn's fiery oratory acted as a magnet to the more bellicose former Spenceans and to those militant supporters of Thistlewood and Watson whom spies called 'fighting radicals'. Included among them was Wedderburn's mulatto countryman, William 'Black' Davidson, now reduced by discrimination and other misfortunes to begging from the Mendicity Society and turning the crank at the Marylebone poorhouse mill.

Wedderburn was now free to cast in his lot with the ultra-radicals Thistlewood, Watson and Preston who had narrowly escaped a treason conviction after the Spa Fields Rising and were resuming their campaign of staging simultaneous nation-wide reform meetings in cooperation with Henry 'Orator' Hunt. Hopkins Street chapel became a 'section' of the new Union with Wedderburn as its 'Captain', and he helped plan several successful mass meetings during the late spring and early summer of 1819. But Watson found the fiery mulatto and his followers difficult to restrain; they urged that radicals attend these meetings with weapons, a proposal which was vindicated dramatically on 16 August 1819 when the Manchester Yeomanry Cavalry inflicted terrible casualties on an unarmed reform meeting at St Peters Fields, Manchester. At the time of this 'Peterloo massacre' Wedderburn was actually in gaol facing a charge of seditious libel, but he was free on bail a few days later when 160 of London's most extreme radicals—nearly half of them Irish—gathered to discuss the news at the George tavern in East Harding Street. Predictably, he was singled out by one of the attendant spies as a 'ringleader' amongst those demanding violent retribution. Watson and Thistlewood now endorsed his idea of arming, though, ostensibly at least, for self-defensive purposes only.

Within a month the London ultras were goaded into abandoning this last veneer of constitutionalism when Henry Hunt dissociated himself from their headstrong leadership, hinting broadly that Thistlewood was a government *agent provocateur*. Wedderburn seemed unperturbed at the ensuing loss of provincial support; he announced at Hopkins Street chapel on 15 September that henceforth the London ultras would continue alone, 'their purpose must be nothing short of revolution'. The national outrage over Peterloo, coupled with rumours of an impending legislative 'terror', made an armed uprising seem timely and imperative. The next few months saw Wedderburn and his followers moving close to outright treason. Samples of spy and police reports reprinted here (12, 15) describe him haranguing his crowded chapel meetings on the urgent need to arm; wooing soldiers with cash bribes and promises of future land allocations; and practising dawn drills with his comrades on Primrose Hill. His followers evidently needed little urging—in order to raise money for arms 'Black' Davidson and a couple of ferocious ex-soldier associates even robbed a man at pistol point near Regents Park. Substantial caches of pikes, guns and ammunition were also secreted in the house of a loyal Hopkins Street follower, leading Thistlewood to declare at a secret meeting on 18 October that 'he depends more on Wedderburn's division for being armed than all the rest'.

Yet as the winter wet set in and the prospect of a draconian government crackdown became imminent, enthusiasm for the insurrectionary tactics of the London ultras began to ebb. By November Wedderburn was doubting the likely success of a mass rising. He warned Thistlewood against self-delusion and gave his own realistic estimate of support as 2,000 at best. Thistlewood's frustrated response was to switch once again to a policy of *coup d'état*; he began planning to assassinate government ministers as a prelude to a general rising. Although the surviving evidence is murky and unreliable, there seems little doubt that Wedderburn and some of his Hopkins Street division were implicated in this last desperate gamble. But Wedderburn at least sensed that the government net was closing in: late night meetings in the chapel ceased on 5 November because news of armed drilling after debates had reached the press and a raid was expected at any time. A few weeks later a spy reported to the Home Office that 'a body of ultras at Hopkins Street chapel, Soho, who are considered as the most determined for carrying the government by force of arms have quarrelled with each other and are broke up'. Under the shadow of the prospective government dragnet some fled the country, some informed on their colleagues and some abandoned politics altogether.

Wedderburn himself did not flinch; on the night the government introduced the anti-radical Six Acts to parliament, he held a crowded debate which ended by urging radicals to tear up iron pallisades to use as weapons in preparation for an impending civil war. Within a week he was behind bars on a charge of blasphemous libel. His followers at Hopkins Street were reported to be devastated; they consoled themselves with the thought that when 'their Black Prince' eventually regained his liberty, he would be 'even more staunch'. Thistlewood, now deeply embroiled in conspiracy, evidently shared their opinion. On the day before Christmas, 1819, he reacted jubilantly to a false rumour that Wedderburn had been freed; '[That] would be one to our strength', he told an informer, 'for Bob always says he will be in the front rank.' He was probably right, for Wedderburn never lacked courage and had declared himself willing to die in the process of 'plunging a dagger into the heart of a tyrant.' Had he been at liberty, he would almost certainly have joined with his countryman William Davidson when he, Thistlewood, and a small band of conspirators met in a Cato Street stable on 23 February 1820 to launch their ill-fated assassination attempt on the Cabinet.[46]

The decision to arrest Wedderburn for blasphemy in advance of the conspiracy is, on the face of it, puzzling. He was watched continually by a bevy of spies and informers, and the Home Office believed him to be implicated in Thistlewood's plot. Given that the other conspirators were coaxed into a deliberate trap laid by a provocateur named Edwards, why did they spring the trap on Wedderburn prematurely? The explanation—hinted at by the Solicitor General prosecuting at his trial—seems to be that they feared his oratory more than his plotting. We have noted that as early as August 1819 the Home Secretary had assured the Prince Regent that the 'notorious firebrand, Wedderburne' would be silenced by prosecution.[47] On that occasion the charge of seditious libel had failed when Wedderburn persuaded the jury that he had been merely engaging in prophecy and divination. The second attempt to silence him was conducted altogether more shrewdly since London juries had shown themselves willing to convict on charges of blasphemy. The Solicitor General argued in court that Wedderburn was particularly dangerous because he preached moral and social subversion to a uniquely low audience.

The spy reports and depositions reprinted here help explain the government's unease. Though crude and ill-punctuated, they capture the charged atmosphere of the twice-weekly debates held in Wedderburn's slum hayloft before a crowd of noisy 'fighting radicals'. They also catch the flavour of Wedderburn's pungent, colloquial language with its hint of a West Indian inflection. He spoke always, he said, 'on the spur of the moment'. Any radical in the Hopkins Street chapel who tried to read from a prepared paper was howled down, just as anyone who attended in good clothes was suspected of being a spy. Yet vivid as they are, these transcribed

speeches tell only part of the story. Like other plebeian orators of
the period, the 'Black Prince' possessed and displayed a theatrical
flair. Bill posters advertised him as 'the offspring of an African slave'
(8); he boasted that many people came to the chapel because of his
reputation as 'a strange, curious sort of fellow.' The radical pressman Richard Carlile claimed that it was this 'powerful eccentricity
of manner', coupled with 'great natural ability', which enabled
Wedderburn to attract admiring audiences despite being 'an uneducated and unlettered man'.[48]

In some respects this lack of education may actually have been an
advantage for it forced Wedderburn to draw on other tropes and
traditions within plebeian culture. His colour, burly physique and
spectacular life story echoed the themes and motifs of popular
melodrama, itself steeped in abolitionist imagery. He also excelled
at radical burlesque and buffoonery, continuing a longstanding
English popular tradition of expressing protest through symbolic
forms. These in turn derived from still more ancient rituals of social
inversion associated with carnival, workshop and tavern. In the
Hopkins Street hayloft chapel, Wedderburn—the black rascal
preacher—and his associate Samuel Waddington—a dwarf
shoemaker—ridiculed the offices, rituals and language of Government and Church in ways that had been practised across the
centuries by Puritan sectaries, as well as eighteenth-century political
jesters like rakish John Wilkes and the radical dwarf hatter, 'Sir'
Jeffrye Dunstan. At some more submerged level he may also have
been replicating West Indian trickster behaviour learned from that
'ginal' figure of his childhood, Talkee Amy, or perhaps imitating the
saturnalian antics of celebrated black street performers such as Billy
Waters—a one-legged 'King of the Beggars', Andrew Whiston—
a lame dwarf, and 'Dusty Bob'—a beggar dustman.[49] The 'Black
Prince' and the 'Black Dwarf' (as Waddington was nicknamed)
functioned as a comic team convulsing their audiences with a type
of mock worship that turned the world upside down for the night.
Observers reported that the throng of young men in the chapel
cheered boisterously throughout, standing 'with their hats on' in an
ancient gesture of popular irreverence also practised by Marian
martyrs and French *sectionnaires*.[50] And, as the reprinted speeches
show, the mood (or 'frame' as some anthropologists term it), of
preacher and audience could switch quickly from the burlesque
to the melodramatic.[51] At times Wedderburn's rhetoric reaches

extremes of passion and poignancy. He presents himself as a literal embodiment of *The Horrors of Slavery*, aiming always to debunk authority and impel political action through shock, pathos or humour.

Perhaps for this reason Wedderburn's fiery extempore speeches contain little in the way of original political theory. Underpinning his violent rhetoric is a typical early nineteenth-century radical critique borrowed from Paine and Cobbett. The state is personified as 'Old Corruption', a set of parasitic priests, courtiers, placemen, landlords and fundholders feeding off the productive capacities of the ordinary people through taxes, tithes and interest payments. His speech in the debate 'Which of the two parties are likely to be victorious, the Rich or the Poor in the event of Universal War' (12) gives a Spencean emphasis to this radical demonology by representing land theft and monopoly as the root cause of popular misery. More typical of ultra-radicalism generally is his outrage over Peterloo, his quasi-republican rejection of a tyrannical monarch, his persistent faith in the press as a revolutionary agency and his artisan anger at the erosion of craft and community standards and ways of living. However, his explicit identification with the 'Jacobins' of the 1790s is unusually bold, even though tricoleur cockades and caps of liberty were making a reappearance in ultra-radical circles for the first time in twenty years[52] (see Fig. 3).

It is in his religious views that Wedderburn appears to offer the greatest contrast to earlier black abolitionists. The blasphemous language in some of these reprinted speeches may seem strange coming from the lips of a licensed Dissenting minister (13), yet it was not unusual within the insurrectionary political culture of 1819. Much of Wedderburn's so-called blasphemy echoed standard radical and Nonconformist hostility to the political 'priestcraft' of the Established Church of England. Popular radicals regarded the Church and its clergy as the cornerstone of 'Old Corruption': through loyalist tracts and sermons, it justified oppression and inequality; it battened on the peoples' wealth through tithes and rentals; and it provided the state with a sinister array of functionaries such as clerical magistrates, reactionary Bishops and zealous organisers of private prosecuting societies. Wedderburn merely gives this orthodox radical critique some real flesh and blood by citing lurid local examples of clerical vice, corruption, and subservience.

His attitude to Christianity and the scriptures is more complex and ambivalent. On occasions he parades an earthy, common-sense scepticism, as when he ridicules such biblical 'absurdities' as the burning bush, or Balaam's talking ass. Sometimes he is deliberately and outrageously blasphemous, calling Moses 'a damned old liar' and 'whoremonger', David a bloody murderer like the Manchester magistrates, and Jesus 'a bloody fool' who 'tells us when we get a slap on one side of the face turn gently round and ask them to smack the other' (13). Paradoxically, all this does not mean that he rejects the scriptures or revelation. Like many of his black preacher contemporaries in North America, he tried to make the bible relevant to the historical and social experience of his audience. He wanted, above all, to relocate its magical authority: from being an agency of popular deference and subjugation it would become a revolutionary sourcebook; 'We should think none greater than ourselves' he roared to his congregation. In the same breath he can assert that 'reason and commonsense' should be man's sole guide, then cite Exodus 21.16 as justification for putting slave stealers to death (9). As an advocate of passive obedience Jesus is called 'a bloody spooney' (12), yet at other times he is exalted as a poor carpenter 'like us', as well as a revolutionary republican who challenged the state in the manner of Henry Hunt and Richard Carlile (13). True, Wedderburn's biblicism has its pragmatic side; he boasts of his extensive repertoire of texts for influencing juries. But for all his 'infidel' reputation, he remained at bottom a radical Christian. The bible was his most basic intellectual matrix and he drew on it automatically whenever he wished to justify revolutionary prescriptions such as armed rebellion, regicide or slave revolt.[53]

The last is a reminder that however embroiled Wedderburn became in English insurrectionary plotting, he never lost sight of the sufferings of his enslaved West Indian kinsmen. His militancy in the anti-slavery cause kept pace with his mounting ultra-radical ferocity. The government first attempted to prosecute him in early August 1819 for speeches at Hopkins Street chapel on the deliberately double-edged topic, 'Has a slave an inherent right to slay his master who refuses him liberty?' (8). The informer whose report is reprinted here was probably right that its real purpose was to urge Englishmen to assassinate their rulers (10). At the same time it reveals how skilfully Wedderburn intertwined West Indian and English revolutionary ideas: he uses Maroon revolts as a model for an impending English insurrection; he likens the rapacity of slave traders to that of cotton masters' enslaving British workers; he links West Indian and British heroes martyred in the cause of popular liberty; and he applies the compelling example of the Israelite rising in Exodus to West Indian slaves and to Britons oppressed by Bishops, Priests, Kings and Landlords (9).

Other speakers took up similar themes; they pointed out, for example, that West Indian slaves were bound to take justice into their own hands because they were denied the right to give evidence in a court of law—the implications for an English working class muzzled by repressive legislation did not have to be spelled out. Obviously West Indian slavery provided them with a compelling local analogy, but most speakers seem also to have regarded it as a burning outrage in its own right. At the end of the debate of 10 August Wedderburn promised to write home to tell his Jamaican slave brothers 'to murder their masters as soon as they please' (9), and one of his handbills reported that the 'enlightened assembly— exultingly expressed their Desire of hearing of another Sable Nation freeing itself by the Dagger from the base Tyranny of their Christian masters.'[54]

The relationship between Christianity and West Indian slavery was the subject of a debate of its own two months later. (14). The topic attacked Wesleyan missionaries for preaching passive obedience to the slaves and for extorting heavy rates from them. Again local inferences could be drawn, but the debate also shows that Wedderburn no longer sympathised with Methodist missionaries as he had done in 1817, perhaps because of the new information that had supposedly reached him from Jamaica in the intervening years. Significantly, he invited two other West Indian blacks to participate in this debate. Like Cugoano and Equiano before him, he evidently kept in contact with members of the local black community and hoped to influence them politically. Informers also noted the presence of other unusually respectable visitors, some of whom objected to Wedderburn's anti-missionary bias and no doubt to his language which 'almost shook [the] room in exclaiming against the church clergy there (sic) Missionaries send abroad' (14). The views of such opponents had little chance of persuading the ragged and violent Hopkins Street audience. Their strong abolitionist sympathies should be noted by those historians who still argue that working-class radicals were hostile to the slave cause.[55] One of the most passionate debaters that night was William 'Black' Davidson; exactly six months later, on 10 May 1820, he was hanged and beheaded for plotting to assassinate the English Cabinet. The following day his friend and countryman Robert Wedderburn was sentenced to two years imprisonment for blasphemy.

V

On the surface Wedderburn's political trajectory during the decade of the 1820s moved closer to that of his black literary predecessors. Soon after he reached Dorchester gaol in 1821, his fellow inmate, the radical pressman Richard Carlile, wrote in the *Republican* that the black preacher intended 'to study metaphysics' in order to further his career as a philosopher.[56] This last was a jocular reference to a series of scholarly free-thinking tracts that were appearing under Wedderburn's name at the time. These tracts were nominally 'edited' but actually written by a supposed Noncon-formist clergyman called 'Reverend Erasmus Perkins', the *nom de plume* of Wedderburn's suave and devious Spencean colleague, George Cannon. The relationship between this solicitor-litterateur and the poor, unlettered black preacher remains somewhat mys-terious. Cannon, an alienated and marginal middle-class intellectual, was no doubt pleased to be able to minimise his own risk by using a man of great courage as a political mouthpiece. Wedderburn's notoriety also increased the popular reach of writings that might otherwise have gone unnoticed. And Cannon seems anyway to have enjoyed acting the role of string-puller and savant to a circle of rough disciples. For his part Wedderburn could experience the pleasure of seeing himself represented in print as 'Reverend Robert Wedderburn, VDM', a scholar, theologian and member of the republic of letters.

Wedderburn's short *Address to the Court of the King's Bench* of 9 May 1820 (16) is a typical example of Cannon's ghosting. Legally this *Address* was supposed to be presented to the court as Wedder-burn's plea in mitigation after he had been convicted but not yet sentenced. And since the jury at his trial had brought in a recommendation of mercy on the grounds of his virtual illiteracy, the black preacher had a real chance to earn a reduction in sentence. Had he used his own plain and moving words, as in the opening passages of the *Address*, the jury recommendation might have carried some weight. Instead, he chose to follow the same procedure that he had employed at his trial; he had a member of the court read out a written speech which had been prepared by Cannon. What followed was no plea for mercy, but a learned exposé of the illiberality and hypocrisy of blasphemy prosecutions. Both the prosecutor and the sentencing judge, Mr Justice Bailey, seized on this as evidence that Wedderburn was no poor, unlettered preacher but the possessor of 'a perverted and depraved talent' who had aggravated his original offence and deserved a particularly severe sentence.

Justice Bailey's harsh words were not inappropriate as a description of the character and literary productions of George Cannon. Two of the tracts issued under Wedderburn's name in 1820–21, and addressed respectively to the Archbishop of Canterbury and the Chief Rabbi of England, took the form of pleas for help in dealing with sceptical questions supposedly raised by members of the Hopkins Street congregation. As with all of Cannon's theological writings, his real purpose was a stealthy unmasking of the crimes and follies of the Christian religion, using a mock-ingenuous tone and a battery of scholarship. A third pamphlet, *High Heel'd Shoes for Dwarves in Holiness*, borrowed its clever structure from Shelley's *Refutation of Deism* which Cannon had earlier published. Like the latter, it took the shape of a specious, mutually destructive dispute between two thinkers—the deist Erasmus Perkins and the Christian Wedderburn—in which atheism emerged as the implied victor.

One tract published under Wedderburn's name from Dorchester gaol in 1820 does seem to catch something of his authentic voice and outlook. The threepenny squib *Cast Iron Parsons* (17) still claims Perkins (Cannon) as its editor, and he certainly polished the expression, but it is otherwise untypical. Cannon in fact inserts an editorial note pointedly criticising Wedderburn for using 'Cobbett-isms'. Its earthy burlesque humour and concrete local detail also resembles the style of Wedderburn's earlier journalism and oratory. We can imagine the shabby mulatto preacher stopping to banter with an old Shadwell apple-seller and seizing on her anti-clerical remarks as inspiration for his squib. True to character, it excoriates the Church of England Clergy for laziness, cruelty and corruption, but praises dissenting preachers of the humble sort for their espousal of 'the meek and lowly Jesus'. The pamphlet also carries a bite of personal conviction when sympathising with artisans and labourers whose skills and living standards were threatened by mechanisation.

These populist-plebeian traits reappeared in Wedderburn's last known and most unusual publication, 'The Holy Liturgy, or Divine Service, upon the principles of Pure Christian Diabolism', which is partly reproduced in an 1828 number of Carlile's *Lion* (18). A reasonably reliable spy claimed that Carlile had some hand in the writing, but the document as a whole again carries the black preacher's distinctive stamp. Indeed, Carlile tried to lend the burlesque liturgy a measure of respectability by describing it as a perfectly serious and rationalist production, though the cheeky title alone subverted his claim, 'The Holy Liturgy' is informed by the same delight in mock ritual and social inversion that had character-ised Wedderburn's Hopkins Street chapel performances. He offers orthodox Christians the chance to worship 'the Majesty of Hell', a powerful divinity whose restoration has been preordained, but who in the meantime is well-attuned to ordinary human imperfections. Interestingly, West Indian folk culture represented the devil, 'Obboney', as just such a figure—a roguish, but useful comic trickster whose earthly powers were widely respected and invoked.[57] As always we cannot be sure whether Wedderburn was here drawing on West Indian memories or on parallel English folk beliefs which likewise depicted the Devil as a palpable and mis-chievous presence within everyday life.

Whatever the cultural sources of the liturgy, Wedderburn com-posed it to accompany a new chapel which he opened early in 1828 at 12 Whites Alley, Chancery Lane. Handbills promised that attendants could for threepence hear Reverend Robert Wedder-burn deliver theological and moral lectures containing 'much singu-larity, novelty and originality'. Abel Hall, a Home Office informer and veteran ultra-radical of Hopkins Street days, reported that Wedderburn intended to compete with several radical deist, or 'infidel', preachers who had sprung into prominence in London during the mid-1820s. Much to Hall's surprise Wedderburn's new chapel did not prove a success; it closed at the end of June 1828 after operating for only a few months. Shrewd as he was, the veteran spy had failed to notice the gulf that separated the elderly mulatto preacher from his new free-thinking rivals. Socially the latter belonged to the ambitious, if uneasy, middling ranks of early nineteenth-century London: one was a former teacher and dissenting minister; another, a successful Mechanics' Institute lecturer; and a third, Robert Taylor, a former surgeon, Anglican clergyman and graduate of St John's College, Cambridge. Operating from substantial chapel premises, they offered lectures on scientific, literary, economic and philosophical subjects to audiences of respectable artisans and white collar workers eager to participate in the twenties' culture of self improvement. At the same time these deist chapels, like the Theophilanthropic sects of France, made a serious appeal to the religious minded by offering a sectarian structure, ceremonial and community life.[58]

Robert Wedderburn and his Christian Diabolist chapel could hardly have offered a greater contrast. Unlike his younger radical rivals, he was too elderly and poor to be able to participate in 'the march of mind' of the 1820s. Despite Carlile's help, efforts to improve his literacy in Dorchester prison came to little, as can be seen from the sample of a letter which he wrote in 1830 (3). The new chapel was actually a converted carpenter's shop which he could not even afford to light. And according to Hall, the 'theological and moral lectures' consisted in reality of the abusive unstructured rhetoric of Hopkins Street days. His audience was composed of a handful of veteran ultra-radicals, most of them desperately poor, or, like Cannon and the Dugdale brothers, decidedly unrespectable. It seemed to Hall, on reflection, that Wedderburn had fallen out of step with the times; even some of his former insurrectionary colleagues had stopped their alehouse plotting in favour of more educative coffee-house debating. The very traits that had made the mulatto preacher such a success in 1819 now seemed embarrassingly unrespectable and eccentric.

Hall's judgement appeared to receive tragic confirmation a few years later when Robert Wedderburn was sentenced to two years imprisonment with hard labour on a charge of operating a bawdy house. The *Bell's Life in London* reporter covering the proceedings found it fitting that a former Cato Street conspirator should now be running a common brothel in Featherbed Lane. But this time Wedderburn's court defence was all his own, and it showed that he had lost neither his old anti-establishment pugnacity nor his flair for Rabelaisian burlesque. He accused one member of the court of himself frequenting the establishment, supposedly attracted by one 'Carroty Eliza' who was usually to be found 'padding the hoof' in Fleet Street. He also argued, somewhat inconsistently, that the

Featherbed Lane premises were used not for prostitution but as a refuge for destitute women.[59]

Given his background in the rough 'blackguard' culture of late eighteenth-century London, it would not be surprising if Wedderburn had been running a petty brothel as the judge and jury believed. In Francis Place's youth such activities had been commonplace and unexceptional, a natural way for hard-pressed tradesmen to supplement their family incomes. These patterns had also persisted amongst Regency ultra-radicals.[60] In old age, as in boyhood, Wedderburn found himself driven by poverty and social marginality to operate outside the boundaries of the law. It was probably the debts incurred from his White's Alley chapel that forced him to turn to the oldest of professions in nearby Featherbed Lane. Had he been convicted of the same offence a decade earlier, it would probably not have cost him much of his standing as an ultra-radical preacher. By the end of the 1820s, however, the permeation of respectable values had changed all this. When one of his radical followers, William Edgar, was convicted of a similar offence in 1829, he was immediately 'discarded' by political associates. Wedderburn probably experienced similar embarrassment when released from prison towards the end of 1831. To what extent he was able to resume his radical career is impossible to say. In any event he did not have long to live; he seems to have died in obscurity around 1835, aged seventy-two.[61] Like most of his immigrant countrymen, and his former ultra-radical colleagues as well, he was almost certainly buried in a pauper's grave.

VI

That Robert Wedderburn died in greater poverty and obscurity than Sancho, Cugoano and Equiano does not make him less significant. Through him, we glimpse something of the tenacity, resourcefulness and sheer joie de vivre of the black London poor. His achievements in the face of great disadvantage warn us of the need to be sensitive to echoes from underground. There is little doubt that this slave offspring, sailor, tailor, prophet, preacher, abolitionist, revolutionary and brothel-keeper left more of a mark then he ever realised. During the insurrectionary postwar years his words and example made the idea of black slave revolution a commonplace in London ultra-radical circles; through him 'the horrors of slavery' became an ingredient in the crucible of British working-class consciousness. His incorrigibility also helped abolitionist sentiments to survive in radical circles during the 1820s when repression and partial economic revival reduced the popular political movement to a flicker.

It was almost certainly Wedderburn who in October 1820 inspired his fellow prisoner, Richard Carlile, to publish an editorial in the famous *Republican* urging the English people and government to take a lesson from the successful revolution of the blacks of Haiti. Though Carlile despised most of his fellow radicals, he admired Wedderburn's courage and principles, which may be why he also included a demand for slave emancipation in his *Addresses to the Reformers of Great Britain*, published the following year. Contrary to the belief of some modern historians, radicals like Carlile saw no contradiction in attacking the domestic political policies of evangelicals like Wilberforce whilst simultaneously admiring their abolitionist achievements. No-one was prouder than Carlile that Wilberforce had made the effort to visit Wedderburn in gaol and had declared him 'an honest and conscientious man'. It is probable, too, that the publication of *The Horrors of Slavery* stimulated popular radical sympathy for the revival of the anti-slavery movement in the mid-twenties. Carlile's *Republican* and Jonathan Wooler's *Black Dwarf*—almost the only surviving radical periodicals of postwar vintage—both published articles at this time exposing planter cruelty and avarice, and both supported the Demerara slave revolt. And though Wedderburn's promised work outlining 'the prospect of a general rebellion and massacre' in Jamaica seems not to have materialised, his radical associates must have been impressed when the prediction itself came true in 1831.[62]

Wedderburn had been one of a small circle of ultra-radicals and Spenceans whose fire was not dampened by the savage government repression of 1819–21. After completing his two year prison sentence, he had continued to meet and debate throughout the 1820s in a series of small coffee-houses and taverns located in the old ultra stamping grounds of Moorfields, Spitalfields, Soho and Bethnal Green. Records of their boisterous political commemorations describe these radicals condemning 'the foul and infamous traffic in slaves', drinking toasts to the republicans of St Domingo and to future insurrections in the West Indies, and singing Cowper's 'Lament of the Negro'. Spies reported that Wedderburn and his followers also frequented the better-known British Forum debating

society at Lunt's Coffee House, Clerkenwell Green, where a new
generation of radical leaders was introduced to republican, free-
thinking and agrarian radical ideas. Details of the speeches have not
survived but we can be reasonably certain that the incorrigible black
orator continued to press for slave abolition and to stress the
identity of interests between black slaves and the English working
class. We know that at least one of the eager listeners at Lunt's,
young William Lovett, developed a fierce hatred of slavery; he also
went on to become a leader of the influential London Working
Mens Association and an architect of Chartism.[63]

Even Wedderburn's ill-fated attempt to revive his ultra-radical
chapel in 1828 had some surprising repercussions. His cheeky
Christian Diabolist Liturgy somehow found its way across the
Atlantic to New York where it reached a new audience in George
Houston's influential freethinking periodical, the *Correspondent*.[64]
And although at the height of the twenties' cult of self improvement
the White's Alley chapel had proved too rough and ribald for
popular tastes, the political climate had altered sufficiently by 1832
for a group of Finsbury ultras to stir radical memories by opening a
'Loft Chapel' which charged a penny entrance fee and dished up
'vulgar' abuse of the Gospels. Even more flattering was the notice
that Wedderburn attracted from Reverend Robert Taylor, the most
suave, learned and popular radical free-thinker in London. Taylor
had written admiringly of the mulatto preacher's talents in 1828; by
the early 1830s he was openly emulating Wedderburn's Rabelaisian
mock sermons. A spy reporting on one of Taylor's packed mock
sermons in 1834 described it as ribald and shockingly impious,
noting pointedly that Wedderburn and 'his school' were also
present in the audience.[65]

Perhaps fittingly this was the last recorded sighting of Robert
Wedderburn before his death. By this time he was an old man who
had lived long enough to see a revival of mass radicalism in England
and an associated resurgence in prestige for his veteran ultra-radical
colleagues. Under their leadership radical chapels similar to Hopkins Street were once again becoming centres of popular political
propaganda, performance and mobilisation. Many of his former
friends and disciples were also gaining leading positions on radical
organisations like the National Union of the Working Classes and
its militant successor the London Democratic Association. This in
turn enabled them to induct into politics new generations of

working-class leaders such as the future physical-force Chartist, G.J. Harney, a young man who acquired both Spencean and abolitionist sympathies.[66]

One of the most impressive of these future Chartist campaigners was William Cuffay, another artisan of West Indian mulatto origin. We do not know whether the two men ever met, but we can be certain that—like Wedderburn before him—Cuffay benefited from the political traditions that had been forged by black predecessors. And though Wedderburn himself died without knowing of the achievements of his successor, he at least lived long enough to witness the partial fulfilment of two cherished radical dreams—the passage of some measure of popular democracy in 1832 and the abolition of West Indian slavery in 1834. This must have brought a measure of satisfaction to a man whose words of 1824 provide a fitting personal epitaph: '... I thank my God, that through a long life of hardship and adversity I have ever been free both in mind and body: and have always raised my voice in behalf of my enslaved countrymen.' (1: 58–9).

NOTES

1. *Republican*, 19 May 1820.
2. The sequence of anti-slavery articles which prompted Wedderburn's letter can be seen in *Bell's Life in London*, 5, 8 and 15 Feb. 1824.
3. *In Miserable Slavery. Thomas Thistlewood in Jamaica, 1750–86*, ed. Douglas Hall, London and Basingstoke, 1989, esp. pp.115, 121, 130, 142–5, 175, 208, 213–14, 216, 218, 221. I am indebted to Dr James Walvin, of the University of York for alerting me to this source and procuring me a copy.
4. See *Equiano's Travels*, ed. Paul Edwards, London 1967; *The Life of Olaudah Equiano*, ed. Paul Edwards, Harlow 1988; Ignatius Sancho, *The Letters of the late Ignatius Sancho*, ed. Paul Edwards, London, 1968; Ottobah Cugoano, *Thoughts and Sentiments on the Evil of Slavery*, ed. Paul Edwards, London, 1969. See also, James Walvin, *Black and White*, London, 1973, pp.102–111; Keith A. Sandiford, *Measuring the Moment. Strategies of Protest in Eighteenth-Century Afro-English Writing*, London and Toronto, 1988, *passim*; Peter Fryer, *Staying Power. The History of Black People in Britain*, London and Sydney, 1984, pp.102–111.
5. James Walvin, 'The impact of slavery on British radical politics 1787–1838', in *Comparative Perspectives on Slavery in New World Plantation Societies*, ed. Vera Rubin and Arthur Tuden, Annals of the New York Academy of

Sciences, CCXC11, 1977, pp.343–67; see also, Seymour Drescher, 'Public opinion and the destruction of British colonial slavery', in *Slavery and British Society 1776–1814*, ed. James Walvin, London and Basingstoke, 1982, pp.22–48; James Walvin, 'The public campaign in England against slavery, 1787–1834', in *The Abolition of the Atlantic Slave Trade: Origins and Effects in Europe, Africa and the Americas*, ed. D. Eltis and J. Walvin, Madison, Wisconsin, 1981, pp.63–79. For the best general context of slavery and anti-slavery, see David Brion Davis, *The Problem of Slavery in Western Culture*, Ithaca, 1966 and *The Problem of Slavery in the Age of Revolution, 1770–1823*, Ithaca, 1975.

6. For a fascinating discussion of how the African experience informs Equiano's writing, see Paul Edwards and Rosalind Shaw, 'The invisible chi in Equiano's Interesting Narrative', *Journal of Religion in Africa*, XIX, 2(1989), pp.146–56.

7. K. Sandiford, *Measuring the Moment*, pp. 24–8, 94, 128–9.

8. I am grateful to Professor David Brion Davis of Yale University and to Dr Michael Roberts of Macquarie University for drawing my attention to William Wilberforce's attempt to convert the radical free-thinker Richard Carlile by visiting his prison cell anonymously and in disguise. See, John Pollock, *William Wilberforce*, London, 1977, p.258.

9. For G. Cannon and W. Dugdale, see I. D. McCalman, *Radical underworld: Prophets, revolutionaries and pornographers in London, 1795–1840*, Cambridge, 1988, esp. chs. 4, 10.

10. Louis James, *Fiction for the Working Man*, Harmondsworth, Baltimore and Ringwood, 1973, p.24.

11. J. Walvin, *Black and White*, p.92.

12. K. Sandiford, *Measuring the Moment*, pp.83, 119–21, 128.

13. Unless otherwise specified, details of Wedderburn's life are either contained in the reprinted documents or have been drawn from I.D. McCalman, 'Anti-slavery and ultra-radicalism in early nineteenth-century England: The case of Robert Wedderburn', *Slavery and Abolition*, 7 (September, 1986), pp.99–117 and McCalman, *Radical underworld*, *passim*.

14. See, for example, a conversation between the spy, J. Brittain, and a group of sailors who attended Wedderburn's chapel, PRO HO 44/2, 14 Feb. 1820, fo. 120.

15. I. D. McCalman, 'Anti-slavery and ultra-radicalism', p.102.

16. On W. Davidson, see I.D. McCalman, *Radical underworld*, esp. pp.53–4, 56, 132, 136, 147–8; Howard Mackey, 'William Davidson', in Joseph A. Baylen and Norbert J. Gossman, (eds.), *Biographical Dictionary of Modern British Radicals: Volume I. 1770–1830*, Sussex and New Jersey, 1979, pp.113–14; Fryer, *Staying Power*, pp.214–20.

17. K. Sandiford, *Measuring the Moment*, p.82.
18. Ian Duffield, 'London's black transportees to Australia', unpublished paper, Conference on the History of Black People in London, University of London, 27–9 Nov. 1984.
19. K. Sandiford, *Measuring the Moment*, p.22.
20. Francis Place, *The Autobiography of Francis Place*, ed. Mary Thale, Cambridge, 1972, esp. pp.20–34, 41–59, 72–90.
21. For an excellent account of London artisans, at this time, see I.J. Prothero, *Artisans and Politics in Early Nineteenth-Century London: John Gast and his Times*, Folkestone, 1979, pp.4–70.
22. Walvin, *Black and White*, pp.96, 101.
23. Arnold Rattenbury, 'Methodism and the Tatterdemalions', in *Popular Culture and Class Conflict, 1590–1914: Explorations in the History of Labour and Leisure*, eds. Eileen and Stephen Yeo, Sussex and New Jersey, 1981, p.30.
24. On such obeah practices and beliefs, see Mary Turner, *Slaves and Missionaries. The Disintegration of Jamaican Slave Society 1787–1834*, Urbana and London, 1982, pp.52–8; Orlando Patterson, *The Sociology of Slavery. An Analysis of the Origins, Development and Structure of Negro Slave Society in Jamaica*, London and Reading, 1967, pp.189–90; Eugene D. Genovese, *Roll Jordan Roll. The World the Slaves Made*, New York and Toronto, pp.171–2, 197.
25. See, for example, Michael Craton, 'Slave Culture, Resistance and Achievement', in J. Walvin, *Slavery and British Society*, pp.112–13; E. Genovese, *Roll Jordan Roll*, pp.210–11; Lawrence W. Levine, *Black Culture and Black Consciousness: Afro-American Folk Thought from Slavery to Freedom*, New York, 1977, pp.43–4, 57, 60; Walter Pitts, '"If you caint get the boat, take a log": cultural reinterpretation in the Afro-Baptist ritual', *American Ethnologist*, 16 (May, 1989), pp.279–93; James W. Fernandez, *Bwiti, an Ethnography of the Religious Imagination in Africa*, Princeton, New Jersey, 1982, *passim*. I am grateful to Dr D.B. Rose, Visiting Fellow at the Australian National University, for drawing my attention to these last two references.
26. A. Rattenbury, 'Methodism and the Tatterdemalions', pp.28–61; John Rule, 'Methodism, popular beliefs and village culture in Cornwall, 1800–50', in *Popular Culture and Custom in Nineteenth-Century England*, ed. Robert D. Storch, London, 1982, pp.61–7.
27. Reprinted in Herbert Aptheker, *One Continual Cry*, New York, 1965, pp.61–147.
28. Pitts, '"If you caint get the boat"', p.283.
29. W.H. Reid, *The Rise and Dissolution of the Infidel Societies in this Metropolis*, London, 1800, *passim*.
30. Cited in M. Turner, *Slaves and Missionaries*, p.57.

31. I.D. McCalman, *Radical underworld*, pp.60–3.
32. See, for example. John B. Duff and Peter Mitchell, eds., *The Nat Turner Rebellion: The Historical Event and the Modern Controversy*, New York, Evanston, San Francisco and London, 1977; John Oliver Killens, ed., *The Trial Record of Denmark Vesey*, Boston, 1970.
33. The best modern study of Spence is Malcolm Chase, *The People's Farm: English Radical Agrarianism 1775–1840*, Oxford, 1988, esp. chs. 2–3; see also I.D. McCalman, *Radical underworld*, esp. pp.17–22, 42–9, 63–72.
34. See I.D. McCalman, 'Anti-slavery and ultra-radicalism', pp.106–7.
35. M. Turner, *Slaves and Missionaries*, pp.42–3.
36. The London Corresponding Society was a democratic club, open to 'members unlimited' and founded in January 1792 in a Strand tavern by a Piccadilly shoemaker of Scottish birth, Thomas Hardy. It consisted mainly of artisans and small shopkeepers inspired by the principles of Thomas Paine and the French Revolution to agitate for political reforms, especially universal suffrage and annual parliaments. It was organised into sections and employed a variety of 'constitutionalist' tactics and propaganda methods until 1797 when, in response to severe government repression, a section of the leadership became implicated in armed revolutionary–republican plots. Olaudah Equiano originally met Thomas Hardy through the abolitionist movement and they became friends. He composed part of his memoir whilst staying in Hardy's house in February 1792 and also joined the Society around this time. In May 1792 he wrote to Hardy from Edinburgh sending his best wishes to fellow members and expressing hope that the Society would continue to expand.
37. On this Spencean underground, see I.D. McCalman, *Radical underworld*, pp.7–25.
38. D. Hall, *In Miserable Slavery*, p.114.
39. On the ultra-radicalism of 1816–17, see I.D. McCalman, *Radical underworld*, pp.92–127; M. Chase, *People's Farm*, pp.78–114.
40. TS 11/200/869, Transcript of Mr Dowling's Notes ..., Examinations of Richard Simmonds, 1–4.
41. See I.D. McCalman, 'Ultra-Radicalism and Convivial Debating Clubs in London, 1795–1838', *English Historical Review*, C11 (April, 1987), pp.312–14.
42. I.J. Prothero, 'William Benbow and the Concept of the "General Strike"', *Past and Present*, 63 (1974), pp.132–71.
43. See *Trial Record of Denmark Vesey*, pp.xv, 28, 46, 59; Walker, *Appeal*, (ed. Aptheker) pp.83–4; Eugene D. Genovese, *From Rebellion to Revolution. Afro-American Slave Revolts in the Making of the Modern World*, Baton

Rouge and London, 1979, pp.8, 14, 49. For a broad analysis of the impact of the St. Domingo revolution, see David Geggus, 'British Opinion and the Emergence of Haiti, 1791–1805', in J. Walvin, *Slavery and British Society*, pp.123–49. It is notable that Cobbett was strongly hostile to the revolution.

44. For modern evaluations of the Maroons, see E. Genovese, *Rebellion to Revolution*, pp.21, 52, 64–8; Mavis C. Campbell, *The Maroons of Jamaica, 1655–1796. A History of Resistance, Collaboration and Betrayal*, Massachusetts, 1988, *passim*.

45. I.D. McCalman, *Radical underworld*, pp.128–30.

46. This account of Wedderburn's revolutionary activities in 1819 is based on I.D. McCalman, *Radical underworld*, pp.133–9.

47. Devon County Record Office, Addington MSS, Corr: 1819: Unrest, Lord Sidmouth to H.R.H., Prince Regent, 12 Aug. 1819.

48. *Republican*, 3 March (sic) [May] 1822.

49. P. Fryer, *Staying Power*, p.231.

50. I.D. McCalman, *Radical underworld*, pp.148–50. See also John Brewer, 'Theatre and counter-theatre in Georgian politics: The mock elections at Garrat', *History Today*, 33 (1983), pp.15–23.

51. See the fascinating analysis of preaching within a contemporary African nativist-Christian cult, Fernandez, *Bwiti*, esp. pp.53–70.

52. See James Epstein, 'Understanding the cap of liberty: Symbolic practice and social conflict in early-nineteenth-century England', *Past and Present*, 122 (Feb, 1989), pp.78–81.

53. For a more detailed discussion of Wedderburn's religious ideas at this time, see *Radical underworld*, pp.140–9.

54. HO 42/192, handbill, 16 Aug. 1819.

55. For further discussion of this subject, see I.D. McCalman, 'Anti-Slavery and Ultra-Radicalism', pp.99–117.

56. *Republican*, 20 Oct. 1820.

57. See M. Turner, *Slaves and Missionaries*, pp.52–3; E.D. Genovese, *Roll, Jordan, Roll*, pp.218–19.

58. I.D. McCalman, *Radical underworld*, pp.188–92.

59. *Bell's Life in London*, 7 Nov. 1830.

60. I.D. McCalman, *Radical underworld*, pp.192–3. See also I.D. McCalman, 'Radical rogues and blackmailers', *History Today*, 38 (May, 1988), pp.12–17.

61. He was alive in 1834, but does not appear in the death registers after 1836.

62. I.D. McCalman, 'Anti-slavery and ultra-radicalism', p.113.

63. I.D. McCalman, *Radical underworld*, pp.196–7.

64. *Correspondent*, 4 Oct. 1828, pp.168–70.

65. HO 64/19, Ball, 17 March 1834. For R. Taylor's earlier
     praise of Wedderburn, see *Lion*, 28 March 1828.
66. I.D. McCalman, *Radical underworld*, pp.200–3.

PART I

The Crucible of Slavery

Robert Wedderburn.

Son of the late James Wedderburn Esqr. of Inveresk.

Plate 1. Robert Wedderburn in 1824. Wedderburn, *The Horrors of Slavery*, 1824. (Courtesy of the British Museum.)

1

Dedicated to W. WILBERFORCE, M.P.

THE

HORRORS OF SLAVERY;

EXEMPLIFIED IN

𝕿𝖍𝖊 𝕷𝖎𝖋𝖊 𝖆𝖓𝖉 𝕳𝖎𝖘𝖙𝖔𝖗𝖞

OF THE

REV. ROBERT WEDDERBURN, V.D.M.

(Late a Prisoner in His Majesty's Gaol at Dorchester, for
Conscience-Sake,)
Son of the late JAMES WEDDERBURN, Esq. of Inveresk, Slave-Dealer,
by one of his Slaves in the Island of Jamaica:

IN WHICH IS INCLUDED

The Correspondence of the Rev. ROBERT WEDDERBURN
and his Brother, A. COLVILLE, Esq. alias WEDDERBURN,
of 35, Leadenhall Street.

𝕾𝖎𝖙𝖍 𝕽𝖊𝖒𝖆𝖗𝖐𝖘 𝖔𝖓, 𝖆𝖓𝖉 𝕴𝖑𝖑𝖚𝖘𝖙𝖗𝖆𝖙𝖎𝖔𝖓𝖘 𝖔𝖋 𝖙𝖍𝖊 𝕿𝖗𝖊𝖆𝖙𝖒𝖊𝖓𝖙 𝖔𝖋 𝖙𝖍𝖊 𝕭𝖑𝖆𝖈𝖐𝖘,

AND

A VIEW OF THEIR DEGRADED STATE,

AND THE

DISGUSTING LICENTIOUSNESS OF THE PLANTERS.

LONDON:

PRINTED AND PUBLISHED BY R. WEDDERBURN,
23, Russell Court, Drury Lane;
And Sold by R. Carlile, 84, Fleet Street; *and* T. Davison,
Duke Street,
West Smithfield

1824.

43

TO
WILLIAM WILBERFORCE, ESQ. MP

Respected Sir,

An oppressed, insulted, and degraded African—to whom but you can I dedicate the following pages, illustrative of the treatment of my poor countrymen? Your name stands high in the list of the glorious benefactors of the human race; and the slaves of the earth look upon you as a tower of strength in their behalf. When in prison, for conscience-sake, at Dorchester, you visited me, and you gave me—your advice, for which I am still your debtor, and likewise for the two books beautifully bound in calf, from which I have since derived much ghostly consolation. Receive, Sir, my thanks for what you have done; and if, from the following pages, you should be induced to form any motion in parliament, I am ready to prove their contents before the bar of that most Honourable House.

I remain, Sir,
Your most obedient, and
most devoted Servant,
ROBERT WEDDERBURN.

23, Russel Court,
Drury Lane.

LIFE
OF THE
REV. ROBERT WEDDERBURN.

The events of my life have been few and uninteresting. To my unfortunate origin I must attribute all my miseries and misfortunes. I am now upwards of sixty years of age, and therefore I cannot long expect to be numbered amongst the living. But, before I pass from this vale of tears, I deem it an act of justice to myself, to my children, and to the memory of my mother, to say what I am, and who were the authors of my existence; and to shew the world, that, not to my own misconduct is to be attributed my misfortunes, but to the inhumanity of a MAN, whom I am compelled to call by the name of FATHER. I am the offspring of a slave, it is true; but I am a man of free thought and opinion; and though I was immured for two years in his Majesty's gaol at Dorchester, for daring to express my sentiments as a free man, I am still the same in mind as I was before, and imprisonment has but confirmed me that I was right. They who know me, will confirm this statement.

To begin then with the beginning—I was born in the island of Jamaica, about the year 1762, on the estate of a Lady Douglas, a distant relation of the Duke of Queensbury. My mother was a woman of colour, by name ROSANNA, and at the time of my birth a slave to the above Lady Douglas. My father's name was JAMES WEDDERBURN, Esq. of Inveresk, in Scotland, an extensive proprietor, of sugar estates in Jamaica, which are now in the possession of a younger brother of mine, by name, A. COLVILLE, Esq. of No.35, Leadenhall Street.

I must explain at the outset of this history—what will appear unnatural to some—the reason of my abhorrence and indignation at the conduct of my father. From him I have received no benefit in the world. By him my mother was made the object of his brutal lust, then insulted, abused, and abandoned; and, within a few weeks from the present time, a younger and more fortunate brother of mine, the aforesaid A. Colville, Esq. has had the insolence to revile her memory in the most abusive language, and to stigmatise her for that which was owing to the deep and dark iniquity of my father. Can I contain myself at this? or, have I not the feelings of human nature within my breast? Oppression I can bear with patience, because it hath always been my lot; but when to this is added insult and reproach from the authors of my miseries, I am forced to take up arms in my own defence, and to abide the issue of the conflict.

My father's name, as I said before, was JAMES WEDDERBURN, of Inveresk, in Scotland, near Musselborough, where, if my information is correct, the Wedderburn family have been seated for a long time. My grandfather was a staunch Jacobite, and exerted himself strenuously in the cause of the Pretender, in the rebellion of the year 1745. For his aiding to restore the exiled family to the throne of England, he was tried, condemned, and executed. He was hung by the neck till he was dead; his head was then cut off, and his body was divided into four quarters. When I first came to England, in the year 1779, I remember seeing the remains of a rebel's skull which had been affixed over Temple Bar; but I never yet could fully ascertain whether it was my dear grandfather's skull, or not. Perhaps my dear brother, A. COLVILLE, can lend me some assistance in this affair. For this act of high treason, our family estates were confiscated to the King, and my dear father found himself destitute in the world, or with no resource but his own industry. He adopted the medical profession; and in Jamaica he was Doctor and Man-Midwife, and turned an honest penny by drugging and physicing the poor blacks, where those that were cured, he had the credit for, and for those he killed, the fault was laid to their own obstinacy. In the course of time, by dint of *booing* and *booing*[2], my father was restored to his father's property, and he became the proprietor of one of the most extensive sugar estates in Jamaica. While my dear and honoured father was poor, he was chaste as any Scotchman, whose poverty made him virtuous; but the moment he became rich, he gave loose to his carnal appetites, and indulged himself without moderation, but as parsimonious as ever. My father's mental powers were none of the brightest, which may account for his libidinous excess. It is a common practice, as has been stated by Mr. Wilberforce in parliament, for the planters to have lewd intercourse with their female slaves; and so inhuman are many of these said planters, that many well-authenticated instances are known, of their selling their slaves while pregnant, and making that a pretence to enhance their value. A father selling his offspring is no disgrace there. A planter letting out his prettiest female slaves for purposes of lust, is by no means uncommon. My father ranged through the whole of his household for his own lewd purposes; for they being his personal property, cost nothing extra; and if any one proved with child—why, it was an acquisition which might one day fetch something in the market, like a horse or pig in Smithfield. In short, amongst his own slaves my father was a perfect parish bull; and his pleasure was the greater, because he at the same time increased his profits.

I now come to speak of the infamous manner with which JAMES WEDDERBURN, Esq. of Inveresk, and father to A. COLVILE, Esq. No.35, Leadenhall Street, entrapped my poor mother in his power. My mother was a lady's maid, and had received an education which perfectly qualified her to conduct a household in the most agreeable manner. She was the property of Lady Douglas, whom I have before mentioned; and, prior to the time she met my father, was chaste and virtuous. After my father had got his estate, he did not renounce the pestle and mortar, but, in the capacity of Doctor, he visited Lady Douglas. He there met my mother for the first time, and was determined to have possession of her. His character was known; and therefore he was obliged to go *covertly* and *falsely* to work. In Jamaica, slaves that are esteemed by their owners have generally the power of refusal, whether they will be sold to a particular planter, or not; and my father was aware, that if *he* offered to purchase her, he would meet with a refusal. But his brutal lust was not to be stopped by trifles; my father's conscience would stretch to any extent; and he was a firm believer in the doctrine of 'grace abounding to the chief of sinners.' For this purpose, he employed a fellow of the name of Cruikshank, a brother doctor and Scotchman, to strike a bargain with Lady Douglas for my mother; and this scoundrel of a Scotchman bought my mother for the use of my father, in the name of another planter, a most respectable and highly esteemed man. I have often heard my mother express her indignation at this base and treacherous conduct of my father—a treachery the more base, as it was so calm and premeditated. Let my brother COLVILLE deny this if he can; let him bring me into court, and I will prove what I here advance. To this present hour, while I think of the treatment of my mother, my blood boils in my veins; and, had I not some connections for which I was bound to live, I should long ago have taken ample revenge of my father. But it is as well as it is; and I will not leave the world without some testimony to the injustice and inhumanity of my father.

From the time my mother became the property of my father, she assumed the direction and management of his house; for which no woman was better qualified. But her station there was very disgusting. My father's house was full of female slaves, all objects of his lusts; amongst whom he strutted like Solomon in his grand seraglio, or like a bantam cock upon his own dunghill. My good father's slaves did increase and multiply, like Jacob's kine; and he cultivated those talents well which God had granted so amply. My poor mother, from being the housekeeper, was the object of their envy, which was increased by her superiority of education over the common herd of female slaves. While in this situation, she bore my father two children, one of whom, my brother James, a millwright, I believe, is now living in Jamaica, upon the estate. Soon after this, my father introduced a new concubine into his seraglio, one ESTHER TROTTER, a free tawny, whom he placed over my mother, and to whom he gave the direction of his affairs. My brother COLVILLE asserts, that my mother was of a violent and rebellious temper. I will leave the reader now to judge for himself, whether she had not some reason for her conduct. Hath not a slave feelings? If you starve them, will they not die? If you wrong them, will they not revenge? Insulted on one hand, and degraded on the other, was it likely that my poor mother could practise the Christian virtue of humility, when her Christian master provoked her to wrath? She shortly afterwards became again pregnant; and I have not the least doubt but that from her rebellious and violent temper during that period, that I have inherited the same disposition—the same desire to see justice overtake the oppressors of my countrymen—and the same determination to lose no stone unturned, to accomplish so desirable an object. My mother's state was so unpleasant, that my father at last consented to sell her back to Lady Douglas; but not till the animosity in my father's house had grown to such an extent, that my uncle, Sir JOHN WEDDERBURN, my father's elder brother, had given my mother an asylum in his house, against the brutal treatment of my father. At the time of sale, my mother was five months gone in pregnancy; and one of the stipulations of the bargain was, that the child which she then bore should be FREE from the moment of its birth. I was that child. When about four months old, the ill-treatment my mother had experienced had such an effect upon her, that I was obliged to be weaned, to save her life. Lady Douglas, at my admission into the Christian church, stood my godmother, and, as long as she lived, never deserted me. She died when I was about four years old.

From my mother I was delivered over to the care of my grandmother, who lived at Kingston, and who earned her livelihood by retailing all sorts of goods, hard or soft, smuggled or not, for the merchants of Kingston. My grandmother was the property of one JOSEPH PAYNE, at the east end of Kingston; and her place was to sell his property—cheese, checks, chintz, milk, gingerbread, etc; in doing which, she trafficked on her own account with the goods of other merchants, having an agency of half-a-crown in the pound allowed her for her trouble. No woman was perhaps better known in Kingston than my grandmother, by the name of 'Talkee Amy,' signifying a chattering old woman. Though a slave, such was the confidence the merchants of Kingston had in her honesty, that she could be trusted to any amount; in fact, she was the regular agent for selling smuggled goods.

I never saw my dear father but once in the island of Jamaica, when I went with my grandmother to know if he meant to do anything for me, his son. Giving her some abusive language, my grandmother called him a mean Scotch rascal, thus to desert his own flesh and blood; and declared, that as she had kept me hitherto, so she would yet, without his paltry assistance. This was the parental treatment I experienced from a Scotch West-India planter and slave-dealer.

When I was about eleven years of age, my poor old grandmother was flogged for a witch by her master, the occasion of which I must relate in this place. Joseph Payne, her master, was an old and avaricious merchant, who was concerned in the smuggling trade. He had a vessel manned by his own slaves, and commanded by a Welchman of the name of Lloyd, which had made several profitable voyages to Honduras for mahogany, which was brought to Jamaica, and from thence forwarded to England. The old miser had some notion, that Lloyd cheated him in the adventure, and therefore resolved to go himself as a check upon him. Through what means I know not, but most likely from information given by Lloyd out of revenge and jealousy, the Spaniards surprised and captured the vessel; and poor old Payne, at seventy years of age, was condemned to carry stones at Fort Homea, in the Bay of Honduras, for a year and a day; and his vessel and his slaves were confiscated to the Spaniards. On his way home he died, and was tossed overboard to make food for fishes. His nephew succeeded to his property; and a malicious woman-slave, to curry favour with him, persuaded him, that the ill-success of old Payne's adventures was owing to my grandmother's having bewitched the vessel. The old miser had liberated five of his slaves before he set out on his unlucky expedition; and my grandmother's new master being a believer in the doctrine of Witchcraft, conceived that my grandmother had bewitched the vessel, out of revenge for her not being liberated also. To punish her, therefore, he tied up the poor old woman of seventy years and flogged her to that degree, that she would have died, but for the interference of a neighbour. Now, what aggravated the affair was, that my grandmother had brought up this young villain from eight years of age, and, till now, he had treated her as a mother. But my grandmother had full satisfaction soon afterwards. The words of our blessed Lord and Saviour Jesus Christ were fulfilled in this instance: 'Do good to them that despitefully use you, and in so doing you shall heap coals of fire upon their heads.' This woman had an only child, which died soon after this affair took place (plainly a judgment of God); and the mother was forced to come and beg pardon of my grandmother for the injury she had done her, and solicit my grandmother to assist her in the burial of her child. My grandmother replied, 'I can forgive you, but I can never forget the flogging;' and the good old woman instantly set about assisting her in her child's funeral, it being as great an object to have a decent burial with the blacks in Jamaica, as with the lower classes in Ireland. This same woman, who had so wickedly calumniated my grandmother, afterwards made public confession of her guilt in the market-place at Kingston, on purpose to ease her guilty conscience, and to make atonement for the injury she had done. I mention this, to show upon what slight grounds the planters exercise their cow-skin whips, not sparing even an old woman of seventy years of age. But to return—

After the death of Lady Douglas, who was brought to England to be buried, James Charles Sholto Douglas, Esq. my mother's master, promised her her freedom on his return to Jamaica; but his covetous heart would not let him perform his promise. He told my mother to look out for another master to purchase her; and that her price was to be £100. The villain Cruikshank, whom I have mentioned before, offered Douglas £10 more for her; and Douglas was so mean as to require £110 from my mother; otherwise he would have sold her to Cruikshank against her will, for purposes the reader can guess. One Doctor Campbell purchased her; and in consequence of my mother having been a companion of, and borne children to my father, Mrs. Campbell used to upbraid her for not being humble enough to her, who was but a doctor's wife. This ill-treatment had such an effect on my mother, that she resolved to starve herself to death; and, though a cook, abstained from victuals for six days. When her intention was discovered, Doctor Campbell became quite alarmed for his £110, and gave my mother leave to look out for another owner; which she did, and became the property of a Doctor Boswell. The following letter, descriptive of her treatment in this place, appeared in 'BELL'S LIFE IN LONDON,' a Sunday paper, on the 29th February 1824:–

To The Editor of *Bell's Life in London*.

February 20th, 1824

SIR,—Your observations on the Meeting of the Receivers of Stolen Men call for my sincere thanks, I being a descendant of a Slave by a base Slave-Holder, the late JAMES WEDDERBURN, Esq. of Inveresk,

who sold my mother when she was with child of me, HER THIRD
SON BY HIM!!! She was FORCED to submit to him, being *his Slave*,
THOUGH HE KNEW SHE DISLIKED HIM! She knew that he was mean,
and, when gratified, would not give her her freedom, which is the
custom for those, *as a reward*, who have preserved their persons,
with Gentlemen (if I may call a Slave-Dealer a Gentleman). I have
seen my poor mother stretched on the ground, tied hands and feet,
and FLOGGED in the most indecent manner, though PREGNANT AT
THE SAME TIME!!! her *fault* being the not acquainting her mistress
that her master had *given her leave to go to see her mother in town!*
So great was the anger of this Christian Slave-Dealer, that he went
fifteen miles to punish her while on the visit! Her master was then
one BOSWELL; his chief companion was CAPTAIN PARR, who *chained
a female Slave to a stake, and starved her to death!* Had it not been
for a British Officer in the Army, who had her dug up and proved
it, this fact would not have been known. *The murderer was
sentenced to transport himself for one year.* He came to England,
and returned in the time—this was *his punishment.* My uncle and
aunt were sent to America, and sold by their father's brother, who
said that he sent them to be educated. *He had a little shame*, for the
law in Jamaica allowed him to sell them, or even had they been his
children—*so much for humanity and Christian goodness.* As for
these men, who wished that the King would proclaim that there was
no intention of emancipation,—Oh, what barbarism!—

———————

ROBERT WEDDERBURN.

No.27, Crown Street, Soho
I little expected, when I sent this letter, that my dear brother, A.
COLVILLE, Esq. of No.35, Leadenhall Street, would have dared to
reply to it. But he did; and what all my letters and applications to
him, and my visit to my father, could not accomplish, was done by
the above plain letter. The following is the letter of Andrew, as it
appeared in the same paper on the 21st of March last, with the
Editor's comments:—

BROTHER OT NO BROTHER—'THAT IS THE QUESTION?'

———————

A letter from another son of the late slave-dealer,
James Wedderburn, Esq.

Our readers will recollect, that on the 29th ult. we published a letter
signed ROBERT WEDDERBURN, in which the writer expressed his
feelings in bitter terms of reproach against the atrocities of the man
he called his FATHER, practised, as he declared them to have been,
upon his unhappy Mother, and who was, as he stated, at once the
victim of his Father's lust and subsequent barbarity. When we
inserted the Letter alluded to, we merely treated on the horrors of
the station generally, to which Slavery reduced our fellow-beings,
but without pledging ourselves to the facts of the statements in
question, as narrated by the son, against so inhuman a parent. But
we are now more than ever inclined to believe them literally true;
since we have received the following letter by the hands of *another*
son—apparently, however, a greater favourite with his father than
ROBERT—and in which the brutalities stated by the latter to have
been practised upon his mother, are not attempted to be denied. The
following letter we publish *verbatim et literatim* as we received
it—a remark or two upon its contents presently:—

To The Editor of *Bell's Life in London*

SIR,—Your Paper of the 29th ult. containing a Letter signed ROBERT
WEDDERBURN, was put into my hands only yesterday, otherwise I
should have felt it to be my duty to take earlier notice of it.

In answer to this most slanderous publication, I have to state, that
the person calling himself Robert Wedderburn is NOT a son of the
late Mr. James Wedderburn, of Inveresk, who never had any child
by, or any connection of *that kind* with the mother of this man. The
pretence of his using the name of Wedderburn at all, arises out of
the following circumstances:—The late Mr. James Wedderburn, of
Inveresk, had, when he resided in the parish of Westmoreland, in
the Island of Jamaica, a negro woman-*slave*, whom he employed as
a cook; this woman had so violent a temper that she was continually
quarrelling with the other servants, and occasioning a disturbance in
the house. He happened to make some observation upon her
troublesome temper, when a gentleman in company said, he would
be very glad to *purchase* her if she was a good cook. The *sale*
accordingly took place, and the woman was removed to the resi-
dence of the gentleman, in the parish of Hanover. Several years

afterwards, this woman was delivered of a mulatto child, and as *she could not tell who was the father*, her master, in a foolish joke, named the child Wedderburn. About twenty-two or twenty-three years ago, this man applied to me for money upon the *strength of his name*, claiming to be a son of Mr. James Wedderburn, of Inveresk, which occasioned me to write to my father, when he gave me the above explanation respecting this person; adding, that a few years after he had returned to this country, and married, this same person importuned him with the same story that he now tells; and as he persisted in annoying him after the above explanation was given to him, that he found it necessary to have him brought before the Sheriff of the county of Edinburgh. But whether the man was punished, or only discharged upon promising not to repeat the annoyance, *I do not now recollect.*

'Your conduct, Sir, is most unjustifiable in thus lending yourself to be the vehicle of such foul slander upon the character of the respected dead—when the story is so improbable in itself—when upon the slightest enquiry you would have discovered that it referred to a period of between sixty and seventy years ago, and *therefore* is not applicable to any argument upon the present condition of the West India Colonies—and when, upon a little further enquiry, you might easily have obtained the above contradiction and explanation.

'I have only to add, that in the event of your not inserting this letter in your Paper of Sunday next, or of your repeating or insinuating any further slander upon the character of my father, the late Mr. James Wedderburn, of Inveresk, I have instructed my Solicitor to take immediate measures for obtaining legal redress against you.

'I am, Sir, your humble Servant,

A. COLVILLE.

35, Leadenhall Street, March 17th, 1824.

As to our Correspondent's threat of prosecuting us, &c. we have not time just at present to say any thing further on this subject, than to remind him that HE is NOT in *Jamaica*, and that we are not alarmed at trifles; so, trust he will summon to his aid all the *temperance* he is master of, whilst we proceed to the task he has himself imperatively *forced* upon us. Our Correspondent, A. COL-VILLE, says, that *he is* the son of the late JAMES WEDDERBURN, and that our other Correspondent, ROBERT WEDDERBURN, is *not so*; that the said ROBERT WEDDERBURN was so called in a jest; and that *his own mother did not know who was the father of her own child.*—All this may be good *Slave-Dealers'* logic, for aught we know—but how stands the case at issue? Two parties say that each is the son of JAMES WEDDERBURN; and, without knowing either of them, the assertion of the one is equally good as the assertion of the other, as far as *bare assertion* will go. But ROBERT states that he was the 'THIRD son' of JAMES WEDDERBURN *by the same mother*; and here we must seriously ask Mr. COLVILE, if such statement be correct, whether he means to tell us that *the whole family was made by accident*, or that the mother herself could not, owing to 'her violence of temper,' on oath, positively swear *whether she had any children or not?* As to the 'foolish joke' of calling a child after its father, we are ready to admit that many a Slave-Dealer would feel himself offended at such a liberty taken with his name; and the more especially where he *intended to turn him into ready money by disposing of him*—a practice with Slave-Dealers, of which our present Correspondent, we presume, is not entirely ignorant. However, if he be in reality, as he says, one of WEDDERBURN'S children, it is evident that the ceremony of calling a child by the name of its father has been dispensed within his own case, of which the difference between the name of his father and himself are striking proofs. But, it seems, that ROBERT WEDDERBURN is not *entirely unknown* to A. COLVILE, nor was he to JAMES WEDDERBURN, 'having applied for money' to them both, 'on the strength of his name'—This matter, as it aimed at the *pocket*, A. COLVILE perfectly remembers, 'but whether the *man* was *punished*'—a consideration of much less importance certainly—he 'does not now recollect.'

But we must now call the attention of A. COLVILE—'the real Simon Pure[3],'—and more particularly of our readers, to the next paragraph of his letter, in which we are informed that we have been guilty of 'lending ourselves' to 'foul slander upon the character of the respected dead,' *because*—what?—why, because '*the story is so improbable in itself*,' and refers '*to a period of between sixty and seventy years ago,*' *and* THEREFORE not applicable to any 'argument upon the West India Colonies!' Although this is excellent reasoning—inasmuch as it has stood the test of *time*, having been urged between sixty or seventy years *past*,—yet it is of that *obvious* description that spares us the necessity of replying to it. But wherein we appear most culpable in the eyes of this affirmed son of JAMES WEDDERBURN, is, that we did not, by 'inquiry,' obtain the 'contradiction,' which we have now so fortunately obtained?—But we are really too busily employed to hunt out the Solicitors of Slave-Dealers' children, for the purpose of inquiring who are so fortunate as to be acknowledged as such, and who are so unfortunate as to be disowned by them.—Yet, after all, the intelligence we *have* obtained by the above letter, is *but* a 'contradiction' of an assertion, *without one single* PROOF that the assertion is untrue.

We now flatter ourselves that A. COLVILE will entertain a more favourable opinion of our love of equity than he appears to have done hitherto? We have inserted his letter, as it was his wish we should do, although we assure him it has not been from fear of any 'dread instructions' which he may have confided to his Solicitor.

One word more, by way of advice, and we have done:— Concerning ROBERT WEDDERBURN and A. COLVILE, each tells us that he is the son of JAMES WEDDERBURN. Slave-Buyers, we are aware, frequently have many children born to them by this dreadful species of female *property*—when the dearest ties of consanguinity are trampled upon by a sordid thirst of interest, we had almost said *inherent*, in the *Slaver*. Yet, let not this unnatural feeling extend to the offspring of such connections—an offspring that should be the more closely cemented by the ties of affection, as mutual sorrows are attendant on their births;—let, then, the bonds of sympathy lighten the bondage to which they were (however unjustly) born; and if PROVIDENCE favours the one, let him strive to meliorate the distresses of the other. A father's marriage makes him *not the less the father of his own children*, in the EYE OF HEAVEN, though borne to him by his Slaves; and we should feel much greater pleasure to hear if A. COLVILE were to *relieve* R. WEDDERBURN (who, by the way, has not mentioned *his* name), than in *his* attempt to prove that a mother does not know the father of her child, and *that* child, as we are informed, the THIRD she had borne to him!

The next Sunday, 28th March, I replied to brother Andrew's statement; and I will leave the reader to judge which had the best of the argument.

BROTHER OF NO BROTHER—'THAT IS THE QUESTION?'

We this day publish a third letter upon this, certainly not uninterest-

ing, subject—from him who declares himself to be the elder branch
of the general stock; and if this be true, we must—*en passant*—in
the first place, address a word or two to the younger scion—a Mr.
Colvile—(we here insert the name as he himself has spelt it) will
perceive by our publishing the annexed letter, that we do *not* 'lend
ourselves to foul slander, etc.' as in a moment of ridiculous
petulance he was, last week, pleased to aver—but we shall hope that
our publication of the little vituperative anathemas denounced
against us in the epistle with which he honoured us, has, ere this,
convinced him how grossly he libelled us in the assertion. However,
we forgive his irritability, and will venture, once more, to give him a
little advice as to his future literary communications. If, as he has
asserted, the writer of the following letter be *not his brother*, instead
of using idle threats of setting his Solicitor upon us, let him seat
himself soberly down in his closet, and send us the result of his
temperate reflections upon the subject in question. Let him remember also, that his argument will lose nothing by *good language*, nor
be the less convincing by being urged in terms not unbecoming a
gentleman. It may not, perhaps, be improper, once more to remind
Mr. Colvile that the publication which first offended him made no
allusion to *himself*—and he must make great allowances for the
warmth of feeling expressed by a man whose natural sympathies
have been so deeply wounded as those (according to his own
statement—and of which he adduces corroborative facts) of Robert
Wedderburn. Let Mr. Colvile send us a statement of *facts* that will
disprove the statements of Robert Wedderburn, and Mr. C. shall
soon be convinced that—to speak in his own phrase—'we do not
lend ourselves to be the vehicle of foul slander,' but are really what
we pretend ourselves to be, and what every public journalist *ought*
to be—*the Advocates of Truth and Justice*. Mr. C. cannot think that
we ever had the least intention of injuring or offending him, aware
as he is that we did not know that there was such a being as himself
in existence until he told us so; and as we are of no party, our
columns are as open to one part of his father's family as to another.

But *Mr Colvile* asserts in his letter of the 17th instant, that the
case therein referred to, as published by us, 'was not applicable to
any argument upon the present condition of the West India
Colonies.'—As to a matter of opinion, we must beg leave to differ
with him: *length of time* is no argument against the inhumanities of
Slave-Dealers, as practised against the unprotected Slave. Many

years ago it was acknowledged that the power of the West-India Slave Dealer *had* been by him abused, but that the condition of his *live stock* was now [then] meliorated. The self-same argument is urged with equal vehemence at the present day; and such *would be* the never-failing *salvo* for ages to come, were the wretched captives to be left to the mercy—we beg pardon—to the *cruelty* of their fiend-like masters: and here we must remind Mr. Colvile that this is not merely our own opinion upon the subject, but was the language of British Senators when commencing the benevolent work of casting off the chains of their fellow men. We would wish to act with *becoming* delicacy to Mr. C. or to Mr. Any-body-else, under similar circumstances, unless forced to cast it aside by him or them—but we say (for we have made *certain* inquiries since we published his letter) that we should have expected that *he* would have been one of the *last* to have spoken with indifference on the *sale* of his fellow creatures. Let us merely suppose that his own mother had been treated as many of the unhappy mothers of Slave-Dealers' children *have* been treated, what, then, we would ask, *must* have been the feelings of any man not lost to all sense of humanity?—And is it not a matter of *chance*, where *interest* preponderates to induce him to marry—*who* of a Slave-Dealer's children is born to him in wedlock, and who is not? Mr. C. has not yet informed us whether or not *he* was born in wedlock, nor do we either know or care.—We will repeat to Mr. Colvile what we have often before repeated, *viz.* our unalterable conviction that the man who accumulates wealth by the blood of his fellows, must ever be dead to the feelings common to our nature. But although we have said we would never cease to exclaim against the horrible traffic in human flesh until there was an amelioration of the condition of Slavery; yet, unjust as is the argument of force against the force of argument, we wished not an *instantaneous* emancipation, although we could have wished our Ministers to have gone farther than they have done, and extended their object to the other Colonies, as they have already commenced it in Trinidad. However, as it is, we rejoice to find that there is a *beginning* to soften the rigour of captivity and fetters; but, as Mr. Wilberforce truly observed, the consequence of disappointed hope might be to drive the Negroes to '*take the cause into their own hands.*' With him, we trust that such may not be the case!

We now return to the point from which we have so far, and not unnecessarily, we think, digressed. The columns of our journal are ever open to redress any wrong we may have unintentionally committed; but we are not to be threatened into silence upon a subject, the truth of which, in some material points, is not even attempted to be *denied*, or *disproved by corroborative circumstances*; and if Mr. Colvile will not follow the good advice we have already bestowed upon him, he would do well to address himself to that Ultra-Radical or Loyalist,—who so jumbles his extremes, we know not which to call him—the *Infamous John Bull*[4].—In *his* columns Mr. C. may hack, cut, and quarter the Slaves *ad libitum*. It is true, indeed, that thus, many thousands of *our* readers may not *see* the ink-engulphed massacre, but perhaps the general carnage may make amends for this deficiency? However, Mr. Colvile will please himself in his future operations; and, just hinting to him (should he address the *Infamous John Bull*) the propriety of passing by the *Scotch Cow*, alluded to in the following letter, we recommend it to his perusal without further ceremony:—

To The Editor of *Bell's Life in London*

SIR,—I did not expect, when I communicated my statement, as it appeared in your Paper of the 29th ult. that any person would have had the temerity, not to say audacity, to have contradicted my assertion, and thereby occasion me to PROVE the deep depravity of the man to whom I owe my existence. I deem it now an imperative duty to reply to the infamous letter of A. COLVILE, alias WEDDER-BURN, and to defend the memory of my unfortunate mother, a woman virtuous in principle, but a Slave, and a sacrifice to the unprincipled lust of my father.—Your Correspondent, *my dear and affectionate brother*, will, doubtless, laugh, when he hears of the VIRTUES of SLAVES, *unless such as will enhance their price*—but I shall leave it to your readers to decide on the *laugh* of a Slave-Dealer after the picture of lust and cruelty and avarice, which I mean to lay before them. *My dear brother's statement* is FALSE, when he says that I was not born till several years after my mother was sold by my father:—but let me tell him, that my mother was pregnant *at* the time of *sale*, and that I was born within four months after it took place. One of the conditions of the sale was, that her offspring, your humble servant, was to be free, from its birth, and I thank my GOD, that through a long life of hardship and adversity, I have ever been free both in mind and body: and have always raised my voice in

behalf of my enslaved countrymen! My mother had, previously to
my birth, borne two other sons to JAMES WEDDERBURN, Esq. of
Inveresk, Slave-Dealer, one of whom, a mill-wright, works now
upon the family estate in Jamaica, and has done his whole life-time;
and so far was my father from doubting me to be his son, that he
recorded my freedom, and that of my brother JAMES, the mill-
wright, himself, in the Government Secretary's Office; where it
may be seen to this day. *My dear brother* states that my mother was
of a violent temper, which was the reason of my father selling
her;—yes, and I glory in her *rebellious* disposition, and which I
have inherited from her. My honoured father's house was, in fact,
nothing more than a *Seraglio of Black Slaves*, miserable objects of an
abandoned lust, guided by avarice; and it was from this den of
iniquity that she (my mother) was determined to escape. A Lady
DOUGLAS, of the parish of St. Mary, was my mother's purchaser,
and also stood my godmother. Perhaps, *my dear brother* knows
nothing of one ESTHER TROTTER, a free tawny, who bore my father
two children, a boy and a girl, and which children my inhuman
father *transported to Scotland*, to gratify his malice, because their
mother refused to be any longer the object of his lust, and because
she claimed support for herself and offspring? Those children *my
dear and loving brother* knows under the name of Graham, being
brought up in the same house with them at Inveresk. It is true that I
did apply to *my dear brother*, A. COLVILE—as he signs himself, but
his real name is WEDDERBURN—for some pecuniary assistance; but it
was upon the ground of *right*, according to *Deuteronomy*, xxi.10,
17.

'If a man have two wives, one beloved and another hated, and
they have borne him children, both the beloved and the hated,
and if the first-born son be her's that was hated;

'Then it shall be, when he maketh his sons to inherit that which
he hath, that he may not make the son of the beloved first-born
before the son of the hated, which is, indeed, the first-born;

'But he shall acknowledge the son of the hated for the
first-born, by giving him a double portion of all that he hath, for
he is the beginning of his strength, the right of the first-born is
his.'

I was at that time, Mr. Editor, in extreme distress; the quartern
loaf was then 1s. 10«d., I was out of work, and my wife was lying in,

which I think was some excuse for applying to an *affectionate brother*, who refused to relieve me. He says that he knew nothing of me before that time; but he will remember seeing me at his father's house five years before—the precise time I forget, but A. COLVILE will recollect it, when I state, that it was the very day on which one of our *dear* father's cows died in calving, and when a butcher was sent for from Musselburgh, *to kill the dead beast*, and take it to market—a perfect specimen of Scotch economy. It was seven years after my arrival in England that I visited my father, who had the inhumanity to threaten to send me to gaol if I troubled him. I never saw my worthy father in Britain but this time, and then he did not abuse my mother, as my dear brother, A. COLVILE, has done; nor did he deny me to be his son, but called me a *lazy fellow*, and said he would do nothing for me. From his cook I had one draught of small beer, and his footman gave me a cracked sixpence—and these are all the obligations I am under to my *worthy* father and *my dear brother*, A. COLVILLE. It is false where my brother says I was taken before the Sheriff of the County—I applied to the Council of the City of Edinburgh for assistance, and they gave me 16d. and a travelling pass; and for my passage up to London I was indebted to the Captain of a Berwick smack.

In conclusion, Mr. Editor, I have to say, that if *my dear brother* means to *show fight* before the Nobs at Westminster, I shall soon give him an opportunity, as I mean to publish my whole history in a cheap pamphlet, and to give the public a specimen of the inhumanity, cruelty, avarice, and diabolical lust of the West-India Slave-Holders; and in the Courts of Justice I will defend and prove my assertions.

I am, Sir, your obedient Servant,

ROBERT WEDDERBURN

23 Russell Court, Drury Lane.

I could expatiate at great length on the inhumanity and cruelty of the West-India planters, were I not fearful that I should become wearisome on so notorious a subject. My brother, ANDREW COLVILE, is a tolerable specimen of them, as may be seen by his letter, his cruelty venting itself in slandering my mother's memory, and his bullying in threatening the Editor with a prosecution. I have now fairly given him the challenge; let him meet it if he dare. My readers can form some idea what Andrew is in a free country, and what he would be in Jamaica, on his sugar estates, amongst his own slaves. Verily, he is 'a chip of the old block.' To make one exception to this family, I must state, that ANDREW COLVILE's elder brother, who is now dead, when he came over to Jamaica, acknowledged his father's tawny children, and, amongst them, my brothers as his brothers. He once invited them all to a dinner, and behaved very free and familiar to them. I was in England at that time. Let my dear brother Andrew deny this, if he can, also.

I should have gone back to Jamaica, had I not been fearful of the planters; for such is their hatred of any one having black blood in his veins, and who dares to think and act as a free man, that they would most certainly have trumped up some charge against me, and hung me. With them I should have had no mercy. In a future part of my history I shall give some particulars of the treatment of the blacks in the West Indies, and the prospect of a general rebellion and massacre there, from my own experience. In the mean time, I bid my readers farewell.

R. WEDDERBURN.

23, Russell Court, Drury Lane.

NOTES

1. Colville here is misspelled, Wedderburn rightly corrects the spelling to Colvile. Andrew Wedderburn changed his name to Colvile by royal licence in June 1814 in order to gain an inheritance through his mother's line. She was Isabella Blackburn, great grand-neice and heir of the last Lord Colvile of Ochiltree. See *Burke's Peerage and Baronetage*, London, 1949, p.2092; Peter C. Newman, *Caesars of the Wilderness: The Story of the Hudsons Bay Company*, 2 vols. Ontario, Harmondsworth, New York and Ringwood, 1987, ii, p.133.
2. booing and booing—making a fuss, a great deal of noise, probably derived from Cobbett.
3. The Real Simon Pure—a hypocrite making a great parade of virtue, derived originally from Mrs Centlivre's tale *Bold Stroke for a Wife*.
4. The Infamous John Bull—*John Bull*, the title of a scandalous Tory and ultra-loyalist Sunday newspaper founded by the hack journalist Theodore Hook in December 1820 in order to attack Queen Caroline and her supporters. The liveliest and most successful of the anti-radical papers, it was probably assisted by government funds, though Hook denied this.

PART II

The Making of a Radical Prophet

2

TRUTH
Self-supported;
or
A REFUTATION
or
CERTAIN DOCTRINAL ERRORS

Generally Adopted

in the

CHRISTIAN CHURCH

by

ROBERT WEDDERBURN

(A Creole from Jamaica.)

'GOD hath chosen the foolish things of the world, to confound the wise; and God hath chosen the weak things of the world, to confound the things that are mighty; and base things of the world, and things which are despised hath God chosen, &c.'

I Cor ch. I, v.xxvii.xxviii

Printed for the Author, by W. Glindon, No 48 Rupert-Street, Coventry-Street, Haymarket; and sold by G. RIEBAU, Blandford-Street, Marylebone

Price Six-Pence

CANDID READER,

Could the AUTHOR present you a Diamond in the rough, you certainly would not refuse it; do not then reject the following essential truths, on account of his unpolished ability to send them forth into the world, with their deserved splendor.

TRUTH SELF-SUPPORTED;

The writer is a West-Indian, son of JAMES WEDDERBURN, Esq. of INVERESK, near *Edinburgh*, and came over to England in the year 1778. Providence casting his lot in a family professing religion, he had a desire to become a Christian; but, hearing so many jarring sentiments and opinions concerning the truth, staggered his mind, and he knew not which to embrace—yet, persuaded it was essential to his happiness, both here and hereafter, to become a Christian, being confident it was the religion of the Bible, which he had no doubt was the revealed Will of God, he had a strong propensity to become one.

A short time after, Providence placed him in another situation of life, amongst a set of abandoned reprobates; he there became a profligate, and so continued for the space of seven years; Conscience frequently smiteing him, and telling him, that the way he pursued was the road to everlasting ruin; to lull and calm these reflections, he frequently promised to reform; but, Sin being such a constant companion, and so sweet to his taste, his efforts and strivings were all in vain.

Passing the Seven-Dials one Lord's day, the author stopped to hear a preacher of Mr. Westley's connection[1]. The words that he spoke, struck his mind with strong conviction of the awful state he was in, both by nature and practice; he noticed, that the minister asserted with confidence, that he would pledge his own soul, that every man, conscious of the enormity of sin, and willing to turn from the evil of his ways, and accept of the mercy offered in the Gospel, the Lord would abundantly pardon; and he was enabled, by the Holy Spirit, to accept with joy, the offered Grace.

In a short time, the author was further enabled to say, 'O!God, my Father and Friend!' and that God's love to him was unmerited —unchangeable—from everlasting to everlasting. At that time, he was perfectly ignorant of the true doctrines contained in the scriptures, and so become a prey to erroneous preachers, who corrupted his judgment before he was able to discern the difference between truth and error; indeed, such was the influence of the errors they taught, that they darkened his understanding.

In this state he was denied the privilege of examining their doctrines; telling him, that if he rejected their dogmas, he was in danger of eternal damnation; but, as they differed so very materially in their tenets, he was confident they could not all be in the right: he then thought it his privilege and duty to admit of no doctrine, however plausible, but what he perceived in his own judgment was clearly and evidently contained in the holy scriptures; not in the least alarmed by the threatenings of the preachers, confident that God had sealed him unto the day of redemption, not only sealed, but removed him by *HIS* power from a legal state of mind, into a state of Gospel Liberty, that is to say, a deliverance from the power or authority of the law, considering himself not to be under the power of the law, but under Grace; therefore, being thus secure, he was enabled with boldness to examine the various doctrines, that he heard advanced at different times.

Persuaded that he is arrived to a state of manhood in religion, and being made wiser than his teachers, he shall now undertake to instruct them, and as they are ready prepared to condemn all doctrines contrary to their own, he does not expect *his* will be very cordially received, yet, he thinks it a duty incumbent upon him to detect error—support and maintain truth, and leave the event to Providence; for he must not fear the face of any man, but speak the word of God with boldness, for, every word of God is pure—he is a shield to those that trust in him, the author will not endeavor to add to his word, nor yet diminish, least HE should reprove him, and then he should be found a liar.

The doctrines contained in the Scriptures, are,

1. Before a man can become a Christian, he must be thoroughly sensible, and believe himself a fallen creature, and partaker of a corrupt nature, in consequence of the transgression of Adam.
2. There is no possibility of escaping future punishment and divine wrath, but by a belief in Jesus Christ, for there is salvation in no other.

By believing in Jesus Christ, the author comprehends ONE ETERNAL GOD AND UNIVERSAL FATHER, in no other sense than as a Creator and Preserver. Jesus Christ the first child of his power.

Revel. 3.14: he is said to be 'the beginning of the creation of God.' The Lord hath possessed me in the beginning of his ways. *Proverbs, c.8. c.12. Colossians ch.i.15.* The first born of every creature. He is also the exalted man. *Heb. c.i.v.7.*

The writer understands by these scriptures that there was a period in eternity, when there was no other Being than the Eternal Jehovah—after this he brought Jesus Christ into existence, and of necessity, he must be the first born—Jehovah, for the first time becomes a Father, and by and with the Son, created all things, and those for the Son, according to that passage, you find *Colossians c.i,v.16.17.* and however he is rejected and despised, there is a day coming, when his friends and his enemies will know—the one with pleasure, the other by woeful experience, that he is possessed with power, by authority of the Father, to condemn the one, and reward the other, and appoint to each their portion, for it is said in Scripture, 'he will judge the world, by that Man that 'he has appointed.'

The Holy Spirit spoken of in Scriptre, is not a Being possessing personality as a Jehovah, but an Influence of Jehovah, which is possessed by the Son without measure. By the purpose and good-will of the Father, the Spirit qualifies and possesses Jesus Christ with the ability of a God, and well-fitted to the work he is appointed unto, so that there is one Will of the Father, acting in the Son, through this Influence or Spirit.—So that this is the Jehovah, the Father, this is the Jesus, the Son of God, this is the Holy Spirit, the Christian is to be baptized into the belief of.

Repentance is the privilege of every man, without exception, for God has commanded all men to repent; the invitation to embrace the Gospel is also the privilege of every man, for the Gospel is to be preached to every creature; and here it is necessary to explain what is Gospel: the Gospel signifies Truth; so that Truth is Gospel: but the Gospel, which every sinner is invited to, is that word of Truth which Jesus Christ brought into the world, commissioned by his Father.

The author does not pretend to investigate the whole of the Gospel, but shall confine himself to a few branches of it. First, That God loved the world to such a degree, as even to spare his Son for their Use; and Christ, who has always one Will with the Father submitted—for their *Use*—for, unless we make *Use* of Christ, actually and personally by faith, we profit nothing by his coming into the world, but are in great danger of having our deplorable state, by our rejection of him, highly aggravated.

The first *Use* we are to make of Christ, is, to believe, when convicted of guilt, that his Blood is appointed, and is sufficient to cleanse our consciences, this being done, our minds will of course be reconciled to God, and our affections drawn out to Christ; as he is the physician and medicine, happy are the souls that are in such a state, for the Oath and Promise of God, and the declaration of Christ, all combine to satisfy their timid souls, that their state is unchangeable, time and place are nothing to them, their future sins can only disturb their peace while in the body, to keep them humble, and at the same time enflame them with a more ardent desire to be at home at their Father's house, where sin and sorrow shall *never* come; this state is called by various names—The New Birth—Passed from Death to Life—Possessing the Spirit of adoption—The Son and Heir of God—A joint Heir and Brother with Christ, and shall share a part of the judgment seat. To judge fallen spirits and impenitent men; in short, it hath not entered into the heart of man, to conceive the exalted state of such a soul, when once happily arrived at 'the mansion, not made with hands.'

A man, in such a state, need not pay any attention to the *Lying Spirit* that is gone forth into the world; by a *Lying Spirit*, is to be understood an influence from Satan upon the minds of men, permitted by the Providence of God, who hath said, 'he will send them 'strong delusions that they may believe a 'Lie, because they receive not the truth, 'in the love of it.' We are warned and exhorted by the Scriptures to 'try every Spirit whether it be agreeable to the word of God,' therefore if any man will judge of the doctrine here advanced, let him take the Scripture for his rule.

The author rejects the doctrine of the Trinity as an error, for the Scriptures assert ONE GOD, who is the Universal Father, and one Jesus Christ, who is the Son and Mediator, through whom, and by whom, the Father performs all his Will, yea, the whole of his Will, by his own Influence or Essence, which is called the Spirit; and if you read the Scriptures carefully, and call upon God in Christ to instruct you, you shall receive a measure of his Spirit, 'for if we, that are evil, know how to give good gifts unto children, much more your heavenly Father gives freely to all that ask him,' pay no attention to any man, but search for yourselves.

Ministers in general, in our day, have their doctrines formed for them—if you go to a Minister of any Established Church, he is obliged to tell you that the doctrine of the Trinity is right.—If you consult a Dissenting Minister, he is exposed to a similar temptation, for if he does not preach the doctrine that pleases the managers of his Church, he is turned out of *his* bread, and held in contempt as an apostate.—If you enquire of a minister of the church of Rome; he is not allowed to think or speak, but as the Pope dictates, and if you should go to the Pope himself, he must of necessity tell you, that, the doctrine of the Trinity is a truth, because it was first broached by the Church of Rome, which pretends to be an infallible Church, and therefore cannot err; so that, according to their sentiments, all that do not believe in their tenets must be damned; therefore you see the necessity of calling upon God for yourselves.

Concerning the works of Jesus Christ being placed to the sinner's account, the Author also contends that the righteousness spoken of in Scripture, which is imputed to the penitent sinner, is called *the righteousness of faith*, not the righteousness of Christ, as is generally supposed. 'Abraham believed in God, and it was imputed to him for righteousness,'—that is, the act of believing stands in opposition to our transgressions, and is now accepted instead of the performances required from us under the Law, or, in other words, believing in Jesus Christ, as the Messiah sent of God, and receiving the Grace sent by HIM, is the only work that God requires of every man.

The writer does not mean that a man merits any thing by the act of believing, any more than a beggar merits by the act of asking and receiving; neither is the act of believing the righteousness spoken of in Scripture, but the Gift he receives in believing; the Gift of the Spirit is called righteousness, for it is said 'I will rain down righteousness,' meaning the Spirit—blessed are they that thirst after righteousness, for they shall be filled—yea, said Christ, on the day of the feast—'If any man thirst, let him come unto me and drink, and he that drinks, shall thirst no more; for the Spirit that I shall give you, shall abide with you for ever, as well as water springing up to eternal life.' The rock that was smitten in the wilderness, was an emblem of Christ, the water that gushed out was a figure of the Spirit, as the water from the rock served to cleanse and satiate the Israelites, so doth the Spirit purify and abundantly fill the soul of the penitent sinner. Furthermore, it is called righteousness, because it dictates to the mind what is righteous, and influences the practice of it; and at the day of judgment, those works performed by the believer, will be acknowledged by the Great Judge of all.

The act of God pardoning the sinner is also called righteousness, David says—'Blessed is the Man to whom the Lord will not impute iniquity,' yea, blessed is the Man to whom the Lord will impute righteousness without works; the Apostle Paul uses similar language, and says, 'we are justified or made righteous, or accounted righteous, freely by His Grace—recollect, that, the word *Grace*, signifies *Free Favor*, so that God has no need of a reference to the works of Christ in the justifying a sinner, though, the sinner *must* receive a pardon in the name or person of Jesus Christ; for it is only through *him* that God has appointed to meet a sinner, and there is *no other* Mediator.

It is generally taught by professors of the present age, that, the atonement of Christ, was to satisfy the Justice of God—the assertion is unscriptural,—they also assert, that, God could not be reconciled to a sinner without his justice was satisfied by the death of Christ—this is also contrary to scripture; the word atonement, signifies *covering*—so, the atonement of Christ, is, for the use of the awakened sinner, who sees himself exposed to the judgment of God, and who would despair, were it not for this Covering, or City of Refuge—it is a fact, though strange, that the Spirit directs the awakened sinner to this DEAD MAN, as an Hiding-place, and there, he experiences such safety, that his fears are calmed, he now possesses a frame of mind, to enquire what he shall do to be Saved from a guilty conscience, then the answer is, believe that the Blood of Christ is sufficient for that purpose, and your consciences though before as 'red as scarlet, shall become as white as wool.'

This is the whole and sole use of the atonement, to deliver the conscience from guilt, that the man may be reconciled to God, to serve him in love—'for if the blood of bulls and goats, and ashes of an heifer purify the unclean under the law; how much more shall the Blood of Christ purge your conscience from dead works, to serve the Living God'—this is the use we are to make of the atonement, and not to trust in it to remove our guilt before God as a sacrifice, suffering death in our stead—the Scripture knows nothing of such a doctrine as an *innocent* person suffering in the stead of the guilty, though it is a truth, that, Christ suffered for the benefit of the guilty; but, this benefit is described under various metaphors in the Revelations—as 'a Tree of Life, the Leaves of which are for the healing of the nations.'

This metaphor alludes to a practice in all countries, where they use the Leaves of certain trees to heal wounds—the Blood of Christ is set forth as Fuller's soap, the wounded in conscience use it, because of its purifying quality—it is also aptly represented under the metaphor of a *Fountain* open for washing away sin and uncleanness, so that the sinner only wants to feel that he is wounded mortally, and that his wounds are become offensive to the Divine Purity, and that he can never be admitted into the realms of bliss, unless he is healed and cleansed; when he feels this, he is glad to flee to this pure fountain, and make use of this Fuller's soap, and there never was one failed yet of being thoroughly cleansed, and obtaining a perfect cure, and, what is more glorious, this precious medicine, and all-healing fountain, are still free for all who chuse to accept them, for they are 'without money and without price'.

Fellow-sinner, you cannot apply too soon, for delays are dangerous, but remember, these remedies are to be made use of *by faith*, for which you must ask earnestly of God, who giveth liberally and upbraideth not.

It is said in Scripture that 'we are brought nigh by the blood of the lamb;' and Jesus Christ died, the just for the unjust, 'to bring us to God;' these and similar passages have all a reference to that cleansing state the writer has above described.

The author has many more well-founded ideas repugnant to the sentiments of the professors of the present day; but, as he expects this work will be warmly opposed, he shall reserve them for a future occasion.

The AUTHOR, in addition to his own sentiments, thinks proper to insert in the following pages, not to break the uniformity of his work, the *HYMNS* of some of the most REVEREND DIVINES; which he leaves to the Readers' own conscience, to refer to their proper places, in the foregoing Discourse.

> Fools in their Heart believe and say,
> 'That all Religion's vain,
> 'There is no God that reigns on high,
> 'Or minds th' Affairs of Men.'

II

From thoughts so dreadful and prophane,
Corrupt Discourse proceeds;
And in their impious hands are found
Abominable deeds.

III

The Lord from his Celestial Throne
Look'd down on Things below,
To find the Man that sought his Grace,
Or did his justice know.

IV

By Nature all are gone astray,
Their Practice all the same;
There's none that fear's his Maker's Hand,
There's none that love's his Name.

V

Their Tongues are used to speak Deceit,
Their Slanders never cease;
How swift to Mischief are their Feet,
Nor know the Paths of Peace!

VI

Such Seeds of Sin (that bitter Root)
In Ev'ry Heart are found:
Nor can they bear Diviner Fruit,
Till Grace refine the Ground[2].

And are we Wretches yet alive?
And do we yet rebel?
'Tis boundless, 'tis amazing Love,
That bears us up from Hell.

I

The Burden of our weighty Guilt
Would sink us down to Flames,
And threat'ning Vengeance rolls above.
To crush our feeble Frames.

II

Almighty Goodness, cries, Forbear,
And strait the Thunder stays:
And dare we now provoke his Wrath,
And weary out his Grace!

III

Lord, we have long abused thy love,
Too long indulged our Sin:
O that our Hearts may bleed to see;
What rebels we have been!

IV

No more our Lusts may ye command,
No more may we obey!
Stretch out, O God, thy conqu'ring Hand,
And drive thy Foes away[3].

———————

1.

Once I abhor'd the Things of God,
And scorned the sacred Word,
At length I heard a heav'nly Voice,
That bid me *seek the Lord*.

2.

Th' Allurements of celestial Love,
The sound of *Calv'ry's* Blood
All the rich Promises of Grace,
Drew my whole Soul to God.

3.

I sought his Face, nor sought in vain;
He did his Grace impart;
I found a Passage to his Arms,
A passage to his Heart.

4.

Wrapt in the Pleasures of his Love,
I'd ever seek his Face;
Walk in Communion with the Lord,
and glory in his Grace.

5.

O Jesus, may I evermore
On thy dear Bosom lean;
Soon may I see thy brighter Face,
Without a Veil between.

HAPPY he who e'er believes,
The Embassy of Peace,
Who at Jesu's Hand receives
The Gift of Righteousness:
God is his Salvation's God,
The Lord is his Almighty's Shield;
He with his Grace shall be endow'd
And then with Glory filled.

HYMN. *The Wisdom of God*

1.

Angelic Beings ne'er could tell,
How God with sinful Man, could dwell;
But the great Wisdom of our God
Open'd the Path in Jesu's Blood.

2.

Jehovah's Wisdom drew the Plan,
How to restore apostate Man;
Wisdom employ'd the Prince of Peace
To save a guilty ruin'd Race.

3.

Jesus came down to dwell with Men,
Their rich Salvation to obtain;
And now in wisdom, he doth cry,
Come, Sinners, to the Saviour fly.

4.

Wisdom's the sure unerring Guide,
She leads us to the Saviours Side;
Points out the Way; in sacred Blood,
And brings a num'rous train to God.

5.

Instruct us by thy Wisdom, Lord,
Into a Knowledge of thy Word?
Make us, O make us, wise to know,
The Paths in which thy Saints should go.

6

Direct us, Lord, in all our Ways,
And form us for eternal Praise;
May we at last with Jesus dwell,
And sing *'The Lord doth all Things well'*.

Holy Lamb, who thee receive,
Who in thee begin to live,
Day and Night they cry to thee,
As thou art, so let us be.

Fix, O fix each wav'ring Mind,
To thy Cross our Spirits bind;
Earthly Passions far remove,
Swallow up our Souls in Love.

Dust and Ashes tho' we be,
Full of Guilt and misery;
Thine we are, thou Son of God,
Take the Purchase of thy Blood[4].

NOTES

1. Westley—a misspelling of John Wesley.
2. 'Fools in their heart ...', by Isaac Watts, *Psalms of David* (1719)
3. 'The burden of our weighty guilt', by Isaac Watts, *Repentance Flowing from the Patience of God* (1707).
4. John Wesley, hymn 340, *The Works of John Wesley: Volume 7. A Collection of Hymns for the use of the People called Methodists*, eds. Franz Hilderbrandt *et al*, Oxford, 1983, pp. 500–1.

3

Robert Wedderburn to Francis Place, Giltspur St prison,
22 March 1831. British Library, Add. MS.27, 808
(Place Papers), fo. 322.

Sir

The Works of Mr. Spence I lent and lost, has to the Bust,
Edwards inform me that Mr. Galloway gave him the orders to make
about fiveteen for particular persons, it appears to me that Mr.
Galloway will be able to give you information, and young Mr.
Evans (Mr. G's nephew) was very familiar with Mr. Spence, and no
doubt will assist you, I was not acquainted with Mr. Spence for
more than nine Months before his death. If you want information of
the fundamental principals of Mr. Spence's plan, and how he came
to conceive it, I can give it from Memory has I was an attentive and
active member of the Spencian society after his Death, but you must
allow me a fortnight or three Weeks to commit it to paper, has I am
convicted to labour I cannot attend to it only at Evening

I remain
Your's respectfully
Robert Wedderburn

PART III

Jamaican—British Revolutionary

Plate 2. Wedderburn, the fiery Spencean leader argues with Owen. 'A Peep into the City of London Tavern by an Irish Amateur on the 21st August 1817—or A Sample of the Cooperation to be expected in one of Mr Owen's Projected Paradises, engraved by G. Cruikshank, published by J.J. Stockdale, Oct. 1817.' (Courtesy of the British Museum.)

4

*The Axe Laid to the Root or A Fatal Blow to Oppressors,
Being an Address to the Planters and Negroes of the
Island of Jamaica.* No. 1 [1817]

Be it known to the world, that, I Robert Wedderburn, son of James
Wedderburn, esq. of Inveresk, near Musselborough, by Rosannah
his slave, whom he sold to James Charles Shalto Douglas, esq. in the
parish of St. Mary, in the island of Jamaica, while pregnant with the
said Wedderburn, who was not held as a slave, (a provision made in
the agreement, that the child when born should be free.) This
Wedderburn, doth charge all potentates, governors, and govern-
ments of every description with felony, who does wickedly violate
the sacred rights of man—by force of arms, or otherwise, seizing the
persons of men and dragging them from their native country, and
selling their stolen persons and generations.—Wedderburn de-
mands, in the name of God, in the name of natural justice, and in the
name of humanity, that all slaves be set free; for innocent individuals are entitled to the protection of civil society; and that all
stealers, receivers, and oppressors in this base practic be forgiven, as
the crime commenced in the days of ignorance, and is now exposed
in the enlightened age of reason.

Oh, ye oppressed, use no violence to your oppressors, convince
the world you are rational beings, follow not the example of St.
Domingo, let not your jubilee, which will take place, be stained
with the blood of your oppressors, leave revengeful practices for
European kings and ministers.

My advice to you, is, to appoint a day wherein you will all
pretend to sleep one hour beyond the appointed time of your rising
to labour; let the appointed day be twelve months before it takes
place; let it be talked of in your market place, and on the roads. The
universality of your sleeping and non-resistance, will strike terror to
your oppressors. Go to your labour peaceably after the hour is

expired; and repeat it once a year, till you obtain your liberty. Union among you, will strike tremendous terror to the receivers of stolen persons. But do not petition, for it is degrading to human nature to petition your oppressors. Above all, mind and keep possession of the land you now possess as slaves; for without that, freedom is not worth possessing; for if you once give up the possession of your lands, your oppressors will have power to starve you to death, through making laws for their own accommodation; which will force you to commit crimes in order to obtain subsistance; as the landholders in Europe are serving those that are disposessed of lands; for it is a fact, that thousands of families are now in a starving state; the prisons are full: humanity impells the executive power to withdraw the sentence of death on criminals, whilst the landholders, in fact, are surrounded with every necessary of life. Take warnings by the sufferings of the European poor, and never give up your lands you now possess, for it is your right by God and nature, for the 'earth was given to the children of men.'

Oh, ye christians, you are convinced of the crime of stealing human beings; and some have put a stop to it. By law, give up the stolen families in possession, and perfect your repentance. I call on a mighty people, and their sovereign, to burst the chains of oppression, and let the oppressed go free, says 'the Lord;' and so says Wedderburn the deluded Spencean. Oh, ye Africans and relatives now in bondage to the Christians, because you are innocent and poor; receive this the only tribute the offspring of an African can give, for which, I may ere long be lodged in a prison, without even a trial; for it is a crime now in England to speak against oppression.

Dear countrymen and relatives, it is natural to expect you will enquire what is meant be a deluded Spencean; I must inform you it is a title given by ignorant or self-interested men, to the followers of one Thomas Spence, who knew that the earth was given to the children of men, making no difference for colour or character, just or unjust; and that any person calling a piece of land his own private property, was a criminal; and though they may sell it, or will it to their children, it is only transferring of that which was first obtained by force or fraud. this old truth, newly discovered, has completely terrified the landholders in England, and confounded the Attorney General and the Crown Lawyers; and what is more alarming, it is not in the power of the legislature, with all their objections to the doctrines to make a law to prevent the publishing of self evident truths, while a shadow of the British Constitution remains. The landholders, whose interest it is to oppose, is driven to the necessity of falsefying and misrepresenting the motives of the disciples of Spence; but truth once known, will dispel falsehood, as the rising sun excludes darkness.

Your humble servant being a Spencean Philanthropist, is proud to wear the name of a madman; if the landholders please, they may call me a traitor, or one who is possessed with the spirit of Beelzebub. What can the landholders, priests or lawyers say, or do more than they did against Christ; yet his doctrine is on record, which says 'woe unto them that add house to 'house, or field to field.' When you are exorted to hold the land, and never give it up to your oppressors, you are not told to hold it as private property, but as tenants at will to the sovereignty of the people

Beware of the clergy of every description, they are bound by law and interest, in all countries, to preach agreable to the will of the governor under whom they live: as proof of which, they must have a licence, if not of the established church. Lissen to them as far as your reason dictates of a future state, but never suffer them to interfere in your worldly affairs; for they are cunning, and therefore are more capable of vice than you are; for instance, one was hung at Kingston, for coining; one in London, for forgery; one for a rape; one for murder; one was detected throwing the sleave of his surplice over the plate, while he robbed it, even at the time he was administering the Lord's supper, in the Borough; and Bishop Burn, of Kent, who had 800 l. per annum, confessed on his death bed, he had practised the same offence for 40 years, and all these were college bred men, and of course gentlemen. You know also they buy and sell your persons as well as others, and thereby encouraging that base practice. This is not doing as they would be done by.

Adieu, for the present, my afflicted countrymen and relatives yet in bondage, though the prince, lords, and commons, are convinced it is a crime deserving of death, to steal and hold a man in bondage.

I am a West-Indian, a lover of liberty, and would dishonour human nature if I did not shew myself a friend to the liberty of others.

ROBERT WEDDERBURN.

TO THE EDITOR

As the present state of affairs will not afford matters of importance to fill up your paper, I am encouraged to hope for your indulgance in granting me an opportunity to contend with all our enemies, who may be disposed to enter into a paper war respecting the Spencean doctrine.

It appears to me very necessary, for it is only by rational contention. that truth is to be attained, It is not right to take for granted that the Spenceans are fools, and mad traitors:—it is their opinion they are wise, loyal, and in their senses, and they alone, respecting landed property. While they hold such opinions, they will naturally be disposed to believe it is their duty before God and man, to preach Spenceanism at all times, and in all countries. Persecutions, whether legal or permiscous, has failed to put a stop to opinions in all ages, whether such be true or false; for it holds the human mind in chains which cannot be broken but by argument. It is my intention to conduct myself in a becoming manner to all opposers.

It is necessary that the doctrine should be stated fairly, that the opposers may make their attact as seems most to their own advantage. The Spenceans presume that the earth cannot be justly the private property of individuals, because it was never manufactured by man; therefore whoever first sold it, sold that which was not his own, and of course there cannot be a title deed produced consistent with natural and universal justice. Secondly, that it is inconsistent with justice. Secondly, that it is inconsistent with justice, that a few should have the power to till or not to till the earth, thereby holding the existence of the whole population in their hands. They can cause a famine, or create abundance; they, the landholders, can say to a great majority of any nation:—I may grow, till, or destroy at my will, as occasion serves my interest; is not Ireland, sufficient to support its inhabitants? Is England able to support its population? The Spenceans say it will, if the land was not held as private property. Furthermore, the Spenceans say, that land monopoly is the cause of unequal laws. The majority are thereby deprived of the power of having a pure government. All reformation attempted by the most virtuous, whether Major Cartwright, or Sir Francis Burdett, or any other virtuous character,— is only an attempt to heal, without extracting the core[2].

To have a parliament, and every man to vote, is just and right; a nation without it, may be charged with ignorance and cowardice: but without an equal share in the soil, no government can be pure, let its name or form be what it may. The Spenceans recommend a division of rents, in preference to a division of lands:—as Moses's failed, Spence's plan is an improvement upon that system which came from heaven. It admits no mortgages; it needs no jubilee.

It is natural to expect the doctrine will spread, and the army of the rising generation may be composed of Spenceans.

Therefore the landholders, who are our despots, will do well to use arguments in time, and convince the Spenceans; though it has been said that the bayonet is necessary to enforce the law; but that will not be used in a bad cause, when men are better taught. The Spenceans say, the clergy must be wilfully blind, or under a servile fear of man, that will not preach Spenceanism; for it is not contrary to the old and new testament.

Spenceanism admits no with-holding an equal share of the rents from any one, not even from a criminal, much less from persons of different political or religious opinions; birth or death is the alpha and omega right or exclusion.

The opponants, however they may be armed with the powerful means of education, whether laiety or clergy, will find that a simple Spencean, who cannot write his name, will receive his opponant as David did the giant Goliah; and with simple means destroy his gigantic impositions.

Spenceanism cannot be confined in a dungeon, if the Evans' are. Hector Campbel, in particular is requested to renew the attact. No private correspondence will be held, while the British government is under the necessity of allowing fortunes to false swearing informers.

To all who love to hear of the increase of liberty, are these few lines directed

The slaves of Jamaica, are ready now to demand a day of their masters, in addition to the day and a half that was allowed before, being taught by the methodists that it is a crime to labour on the sabbath day; and it is the opinion of many, that they will have it.

This information is by my brother's wife, who is held as a slave by a clergyman of the church of England; whether she obtained this information from the conversation which passed at her master's table, or whether it is her own observation, on what she had heard among her fellow slaves, I will not avow; but this information is confirmed by a letter from a book-keeper to his mother, who informed me, that it is the opinion of her son, that the island of

Jamaica will be in the hands of the blacks within twenty years. Prepare for flight, ye planters, for the fate of St. Domingo awaits you. Get ready your blood hounds, the allies which you employed against the Maroons. Recollect the fermentation will be universal. Their weapons are their bill-hooks; their store of provision is every were in abundance; you know they can live upon sugar canes, and a vast variety of herbs and fruits,—yea, even upon the buds of trees. You cannot cut off their supplies. They will be victorious in their flight, slaying all before them; they want no turnpike roads: they will not stand to engage organised troops, like the silly Irish rebels. Their method of fighting is to be found in the scriptures, which they are now learning to read. They will slay man, woman, and child, and not spare the virgin, whose interest is connected with slavery, whether black, white, or tawny. O ye planters, you know this has been done; the cause which produced former bloodshed still remains,—of necessity similar effects must take place. The holy alliance of Europe, cannot prevent it, they have enough to do at home, being compelled to keep a standing army in the time of peace, to enforce the civil law.

My heart glows with revenge, and cannot forgive. Repent ye christians, for flogging my aged grandmother before my face, when she was accused of witchcraft by a silly European. O Boswell, ought not your colour and countrymen to be visited with wrath, for flogging my mother before my face, at the time when she was far advanced in pregnancy. What was her crime? did not you give her leave to visit her aged mother; (she did not acquaint her mistress at her departure,) this was her fault. But it originates in your crime in holding her as a slave—could not you wait till she returned, but travel 15 miles to punish her on that visit. You set a pattern to your slaves to treat your wife with contempt, by taking your negro wenches to your adultrous bed, in preference to your wedded wife. It being a general practice in the island, is no excuse for you,—who was a scholar and professed to be a christian—how can I forgive you? Oh! my father, what do you deserve at my hands? Your crimes will be visited upon your legitimate offspring: for the sins of a wicked father will be visited upon his children, who continues in the practice of their father's crimes. Ought I not to encourage your slaves, O my brother, to demand their freedom even at the danger of your life, if it could not be obtained without. Do not tell me you hold them by legal right. No law can be just which deprives another of his liberty, except for criminal offences: such law-makers according to the rules of equity, are felons of the deepest dye; for they attempt to justify wickedness. The time is fast approaching, when such rulers must act righteously, or be drawn from their seats; for truth and justice must prevail—combined armies cannot stop their progress—religious superstition, the support of tyrants, gives way.

The priesthood who took the lead, are compelled to sculk in the rear, and take shelter under Bell's system of education, to impress on the minds of youth their nonsensical creed; dreading the purity of the Lancasterian mode. But you my countrymen, can act without education; the equality of your present station in slavery, is your strength. You all feel the injury—you are all capable of making resistance. Your oppressors know—they dread you—they can foresee their downfal when you determine to obtain your liberty, and possess your natural right—that is freedom. Beware, and offend not your God, like the jews of old, in choosing a king; agrandise no man by forms of law. He who preserves your liberty, will of necessity receive universal praise, like Washington, to endless generations, without the aid of hireling priests to celebrate his fame.

Check if possible by law and practice, that avarice in man, which is never satisfied. If you suffer any among you to become emensly rich, he will want homage, and a title; yea, he will dispose of your lives, liberty, and property; and to support his divine right, he will establish a priesthood—he will call in foreign usurpers to assist him to oppress you. Under the protection of foreign bayonets, he will threaten to erect a gallows at every door. France is reduced to this state of humiliation. A black king is capable of wickedness, as well as a white one.

WEDDERBURN.

NOTES

1. Spy records, etc, etc, leave no doubt that Wedderburn was the editor of *Axe*. There are two possible explanations for this reference, the first, is that he is trying to create the impression that the periodical was more than a one man operation, that there was a community of readers, contributors and pressmen involved in the production of the work; the second is that this is some of the material transferred over from a predecessor journal, *Forlorn Hope*, which he ran with the assistance of another Spencean, Charles Jennison.

2. Major John Cartwright (1740–1824) was a much respected
   veteran radical best known for his countrywide tour of 1811
   to set up Hampden reform clubs. He was a consistent
   advocate of universal suffrage, and is often accredited with
   having originated the six points of the Peoples' Charter. Sir
   Francis Burdett (1770–1844) became known as a champion of
   popular liberty when serving as an independent MP during
   the 1790s, campaigning vigorously against government corruption and anti-democratic repression. He was elected to the
   relatively democratic seat of Westminster in 1807 and took
   up a variety of oppositionist and radical causes. Although
   moderate in his reform aims, he was not afraid to associate
   with extremists and revolutionaries, including members of the
   United Irish and United English underground.

5

The Axe Laid to the Root No. 2 [1817]

ADDRESS TO THE SLAVES OF JAMAICA

DEAR COUNTRYMEN,

It is necessary for you to know how you may govern yourselves without a king, without lords, dukes, earls, or the like; these are classes of distinction which tend only to afflict society. I would have you know, with all the proud boasting of Europeans they are yet ignorant of what political liberty is: the Britons boast of the perfection of their free government, and excellent constitution, and yet they are constantly finding fault with their rulers. You would hardly think it possible that tens of thousands of Englishmen, would give their votes to elect a Member, for a cheap dinner, and a day's drunkenness, others for a few pounds, some for promises of future rewards, and yet take a solemn oath that they gave their vote freely, and the person they voted for is the man of their choice. Many of them know, at the same time, that they are telling lies. If all liars and false swearers were struck dead at this period there would be but few voters left: The government of England was founded on principles of liberty, and it is said, its constitution is the work of a wise and brave people, who, considering that all power was derived from them, and was to be subservient to their happiness. After they had formed this constitution, and recovered, by their exertion their liberty, they had not sense to keep it, they placed it into the hands of those they called their three States, then their freedom ceased that is to say, they.chose three masters. These three, when they agree, may dispose of their lives and properties. Britons, where is your liberty now? Why, it is in the hands of your governors, you have made them omnipotent, they can do any thing; they can make bastards lawful; they can dissolve marriages, and, at the same time say, whoever God or the Established Priests has joined together, no man shall separate; they can make a child of one year old twenty one by saying so; they can make right wrong, or wrong right; they punish in this country for stealing of children though the thief be rich, and intends the child to inherit his estates; and, at the same time, they make it right that hundreds of thousands of Africans may be stolen, and sold, like cattle, in the market; in truth, they can do, what is impossible for God to do. I have mentioned these things, my countrymen, to warn you against this mode of governing, it being absurd and ridiculous. You might expect, that I should point out a form of government for you, this I leave to your judgment; but my opinion is, the foundation of your government should be this, that every thing should be settled by votes throughout your nation. Should Experience prove the first majority wrong, Necessity will compel you to pole the second time: the public will is easy attained by that mode, and Class youselves in divisions, chuse a delegate to represent you, one for every 2,000, change them once a year, let ten years elapse before you send the same person again: a continual change will improve and qualify many of you, to understand your laws and customs, and check that tyranny which is natural to man. Have no white delegate in your assembly, never have a man worth more than five hundred a year: all laws framed by your assembly, must be sanctioned by a majority of votes throughout the nation. Put no man to death for any crime, flog no body after fourteen years of age, nor cut off the nose nor ears, as is the practice in Jamaica. Let there be state caps, marked with the different crimes, whether it be murder, false-swearing, etc. Let each criminal, after a trial by jury, wear the cap which describes his crime; murder, for life, others in proportion to their guilt: he who attempts to take a man's life away falsely should be deemed a murderer. Let the cap be secure as a helmet. Let no man be pardoned who breaks your laws, let every individual learn the art of war, yea, even the females, for they are capable of displaying courage. You will have need of all your strength to defend yourself against those men, who are now scheming in Europe against the blacks of St. Domingo. Teach your children these lines, let them be sung on the Sabbath day, in remembrance of your former sufferings, which will show you what you may expect from the hands of European Christians, by what they have practised before.

The Desponding Negro

ON Afric's wide plains where the lion now roaring,
When freedom stalks forth the vast desert exploring,
I was dragg'd from my hut and enchain'd as a slave,
In a dark floating dungeon upon the salt wave.

CHORUS

Spare a half-penny, spare a half penny,
O spare a half,penny to a poor Negro boy.
Toss'd on the wide main, I all wildly despairing
Burst my chains, rush'd on deck with my eye balls wide
　　glaring,
When the light'ning's dread blast, struck the inlets of day,
And its glorious bright beam sent for ever away.

　　Spare, etc.

The despoiler of man his prospect thus losing
Of gain by my sale, not a blind bargain chusing,
As my value compar'd with my keeping was light,
Had me dash'd overboard in the dead of the night.

　　Spare, etc.

And, but for a bark, to Britannia's coast bound then,
All my cares by that plunge in the deep had been drown'd
　　then,
But by moonlight deferred was dash'd from the wave,
And reluctantly robb'd of a watery grave.

　　Spare, &c.

How disastrous my fate, freedom's ground though I tread
　　now,
Torn from home, wife and children, I wander for bread now,
While seas roll between us which ne'er can be cross'd,
And hope's distant glimmering in darkness is lost.

　　Spare, &c.

But of minds foul and fair, when the judge and the ponderer,
Shall restore light and rest to the blind and the wanderer,
The European's deep dye may out-rival the foe,
And the soul of an Ethiop prove whiter than snow.

Spare, &c.

The Negro Boy sold for a Watch

WHEN thirst of gold enslaves the mind,
 And selfish views alone bear sway,
Man turns a savage to his kind,
 And blood and rapine mark the way,
  Alas! for this poor simple toy,
  I sold the weeping negro boy.

His father's hope, his mother' pride,
 Tho' black, yet comely to their view,
I tore him helpless from their side,
 I gave him to a ruffian crew,
  To fiends that Afric's coast annoy,
  I sold the weeping negro boy.

In isles that deck the western waves,
 The unhappy youth was doom'd to dwell,
A poor forlorn insulted slave.
 A beast that Christians buy and sell,
  And yet for this same simple toy,
  I sold the weeping negro boy.

May he who walks upon the wind,
 Whose voice in thunder's heard on high,
Who doth the raging tempest bind,
 And wings the lightening thro' the sky,
  Forgive the wretch, who, for a toy,
  Could sell the guiltless negro boy.

Let every male and female be provided with instruments of war,
at the age of 18. Like the industrious bee, protect your hive, drive

out the drones, let no one live amongst you, who contributes not to the welfare of the state; he that will not labour in body or mind, let him not eat, says the apostle: the word of God is, thou shalt get thy bread by the sweat of thy brow. The founders of Christianity have set you a pattern, Paul laboured with his hands. Should the quakers or any other religious sect forbid you using the sword, put them in the front of the battle, as David did Uria: he that will not contend for his liberty is not worthy of it. Have no lawyers amongst you, they cannot be honest in their profession; have no barracks, but keep your arms and ammunition in your own possession. Appoint inspectors to see that all are provided; have no prisons, they are only schools for vice, and depots for the victims of tyranny; appoint a fools-cap to be worn at the age of five, by every one who knows not the alphabet; let the females be the teachers, till the children can read and write; appoint a cap of wisdom, expressing on it the degree of improvement to which the child has attained; this will cause emulation in the youth and parents, to cast away the cap of ignorance; wear the cap of wisdom to the age of fourteen. Let the alphabet be engraven on your trees, and on every public wall, for knowledge is god-like strength, which will regulate your physical force. Bribe no one to serve the public. For glory and immortal fame will perpetuate the remembrance of the hero to endless generations.—That is a sufficient reward.

In some countries the law is spun to an invisible thread, framed in language the vulgar cannot understand. The judges cannot comprehend it, they vary in opinion. The means to obtain justice is so expensive, that justice cannot be obtained by the poor; there are many in England who gain a livelihood by laying legal traps to slay the ignorant poor for reward, and with all, the innumerable laws that are in being, there is not one to punish these legal murderers. They have the interest of the rich at their heart; therefore, I advise you to be aware of the rich, for they hate the poor, says 'Solomon.' Again I say, have no lawyers amongst you, every dispute may be decided in your own villages, by 12 men and 12 women; let them be above fifty; do not despise the judgment of old women, for they are generally clear in their perceptions. Let them be chosen from the adjoining village, should they give a wrong decision, they will only be like the refined Europeans, who, frequently in their courts of law, let the guilty escape, and punish the supporters of justice and truth. Administer no oath amongst you, it is all a deception, honest persons do not need it, a rogue cannot be bound by it. If you discover any amongst you giving false evidence wilfully, let him wear a criminal's cap for life, with this inscription on it—I AM A LIAR.

Pardon no man, for it is an indirect violation of law, and a positive perversion of justice, it is a fludgate to corruption; let your delegates be judges, to try all cases of magnitude in the house of assembly, and for convenience and accuracy, let evidence of the case be taken on the spot, where the crime was committed; a jury in the village ought to take down the evidence, let it be sealed up, and sent to the assembly, there to be decided. This method of proceeding will prevent inconveniency and expence; for thousands have been ruined in the process towards a trial, and afterwards been proved innocent. The system that admits of this wretched practice, of necessity, must afflict the innocent. The lawyers in England drink a health to the glorious uncertainty of the law: they may be compared to tricking gamblers, playing at the game of pricking in the garter. This game will always be carried on while the great manage the law, and the younger son is deprived of a share of his father's estate you must know, that in this country, the eldest son gets the whole, and the others are turned on the public; he that is wild or ungovernable is trained for war, he that is crafty and can out-wit his play-mates and companions is brought up to the law; but, if there should be a third who discovers little or no sense, he will, notwithstanding, be inclined to piety, he is made a parson of; therefore you see the necessity for war, for imperfect laws and church establishment, so that all the sons of the rich may be provided for.

                                                                    R.W.

The Africans Complaint on board a Slave Ship.

TREMBLING, naked, wounded, sighing,
    On dis wi[n]ged house I stand,
Dat with poor black man is flying,
    far away from his own land.

Fearful water all aro[u]nd me!
    Strange de sight on every hand,
Hurry, noise, and shouts confound me,
    When I look for Negro land.

Every thing I see affrights me,
  Nothing I can understand,
With de scourges white man fight me,
  None of dis in Negro land.

Here de white man beat de black man,
  'Till he's sick and cannot stand,
Sure de black be eat by white man,
  Will not go to white man's land.

Here in chains poor black man lying,
  Put so tick, dey on us stand,
Ah! with heat and smells wer'e dying,
  'Twas not dus in Negro land.

Dere w've room and air and freedom
  Dere our little dwellings stand,
Families, and rice to feed 'em,
  Oh! I weep for Negro land.

Joyful dere before de doors.
  Play our children hand in hand;
Fresh de fields, and sweet de flow'rs,
  Green de hills in Negro land.

Dere I often go when sleeping,
  See my kindred round me stand,
Hear 'em toke—den wak in weeping,
  Dat I've lost my Negro land.

Dere my black love arms were round me,
  De whole night, not like dis band,
Close dey held, but did not wound me,
  Oh! I die for Negro land.

De had traders stole and sold me,
  Den was put in iron band,
When I'm dead they cannot hold me,
  Soon I'll be in black man land.

6

The Axe Laid to the Root No. 4 [1817]

DEAR MISS CAMPBELL[1],

WHEN I heard of your kindness to my aged mother, it affected my whole frame, and made such an impression on my mind that I was at a loss to know which way to make you amends, but I soon accused myself for such a thought, when I recollected that it was a West Indian that performed the deed, who knows no merit in doing acts of humanity: but, how was I struck with wonder and astonishment, when John, our brother, described to me your manner and action when you went to your drawer and took the record and presented it to him, saying, here, John, take your freedom. What you then performed is beyond the power of princes to imitate. Oh! Miss Campbell, the greatness of the deed has inspired me with a zeal to extend freedom beyond present conception: Yes, the slaves shall be free, for a multiplied combination of ideas, which amount to prophetic inspiration and the greatness of the work that I am to perform has influenced my mind with an enthusiasm, I cannot support: I must give vent, I have commenced my carear, the press is my engine of destruction. I come not to make peace; my fury shall be felt by princes, bidding defiance to pride and prejudice. Truth is my arrow stained with Africans' blood, rendered poisonous by guilt, while they hold my innocent fellow as a slave, I will kindle wrath in their inmost souls which the eternal God himself, whose throne is founded on the bed of justice, will not be willing to take away until they make a public confession, and give up the stolen Africans now in their possession. An act of Parliament will not afford a cover for their guilty heads, for the makers of unjust laws throughout the earth are in a state of condemnation. Fast bound by eternal truth, I have hold of the God of Israel, like a Jacob, and will not let him go. I will be made a prince by prevailing, though a halter be about my neck. Jacob, I will excell you in proportion to the present improved state of society. Miss Campbell, though a goddess, I have a command for thee to obey: like the Christians of old, you have fallen from the purity of the Maroons, your original, who fought for twenty years against the Christians, who wanted to reduce them again to slavery, after they had fled into the woods from the Spaniards. Yes, the English, in the days of Cromwell, while they were asserting the rights of man at home, were destroying your ancestors then fighting for their liberty; but the Calamantees, as the late Pitt declared, in the House of Commons, led to victory, other tribes less valiant. They were reckoned worth five pounds per head, or each pair of ears; this was the price the Christians bid for your forefathers. The Maroons were not barbarous, nor voracious; this was proved by a bold flag of truce, whose name, I am sorry to say, I cannot recollect; but he was such a character as their present governor, the Duke of Manchester. The Maroons were human beings, and ought not to be hunted down by Britons acting the blood-hound's part. Yes, Miss Campbell, this mediator, I can give him no greater name, he went to the woods without protection excepting that of the generous negro to whom he went. There was not a London assassin with a bloody dagger to give a criminal stab, as was done to Wat Tyler. A treaty was agreed to on the spot, without a written document, which exists to this day, by verbal tradition; but more of this hereafter.

Now, my Dear Miss Campbell, be not alarmed or surprised, though you hold slaves, they must be let free, tho' sanctioned by the laws of England, agreeable to the laws of Spain. Your property is in them you say: the Spaniards had the same wicked supposed right in you, and all your property, by that original base law of slaveholding; besides, you cannot hold them long. I will inform you for your present safety, and for the future good of your offspring, to let the slaves go free immediately, for in their prison house a voice is heard, loose him and let him go.

Chuse ye, as Moses said to the Jews, I have given you time to consider. Have you decided? Yes, I have. My conclusion is this, a mind free from guilt is a heaven on earth. Human nature wants but little, nor that little long. I will trust to the sympathy of nature's universal law, then call your slaves together, let them form the half circle of a new moon, tell them to sit and listen to the voice of truth, say unto them, you who were slaves to the cruel Spaniards stolen from your country, and brought here, but Cromwell, the great, who humbled kings at his feet, and brought one to the scaffold, sent a fleet out, whose admiral dared not return without performing something to please his master. Came here and drove the Spaniards out; the slaves, my people, then fled to the woods for refuge, the invaders called to them to return to bondage, they refused; they contended for twenty years, and upwards; bondage was more terrific than death. At last, a wise and good man appeared from England, and ventured amongst them without a guard, proposed a treaty of peace, agreeable to their own will, which they agreed to. Here, you see my origin, and the cause of my freedom, but I have been tempted to purchase you as slaves, by the example of the white men, who are sanctioned by the English government, being void of shame. I am now instructed by a child of nature, to resign to you your natural right in the soil on which you stand, agreeable to Spence's plan. You are no longer slaves my conscience is free from guilt, but the blood of my ancestors, who fell for freedom's cause will be required at the hands of the white men, who, against knowledge, refuse obedience to nature's law, The unexpected sound, you are no longer slaves, deprived them of speech; some fainted with joy, the rest were amazed, an old man, whose head was white as snow, cried out, Lord help us! Missy, Missy, you sall sit on de same seat wid de Virgin Mary; may God make dee his servant. I will go to toder country in peace. He then dropped, like Palmer[2], on the stage: by this time, the rest of the slaves recovered from their stupor, four young men with solemn respect, bore the corpse away The slaves seemed all disposed to speak at once. Oh! Missy, good Missy, good Missy, what me do for you, proceeded from all their tongues. Oh! says Miss Campbell, I have enough to be done by you all, I have afflicted many of you for crimes produced by the slavish system of oppression.

Oh! Elizabeth, who first sanctioned the inhuman traffic, canst thou take away my guilt? No, cried a voice from some invisible being, the people should have resisted inhuman laws when proposed. Princes cannot help you, they have guilt enough, they can hardly answer for their own iniquities. In tophit voices are heard: Behold the man who gave fortunes to swear away the lives of men, to keep them on their blood stained thrones, is now become like one

of us. Oh! Lucifer, son of Corruption, who art fallen, is it thou who
made the earth to tremble. Miss Campbell being well acquainted
with the scriptures, recollected a passage that relieved her mind,
which was, confess your sins, one to the other, and be forgiven: she
then addressed herself to the negros, in these words; I appeal to the
simplicity of your nature; forgive me, I have the written word of
God to plead in my behalf: you are commanded to forgive—I
confess my guilt—I have given up the wicked claim. The slaves cried
out, Oh! What me forgive? You was always good, missy, missy, we
will live wid you—we no go away. Miss Campbell then cried, the
land is yours, not because Wedderburn, the Spencean says so, for I
have read the word of God, and it says, the Lord gave the earth to
the children of men. You are the children of men as well as others.
I can show no title deeds that are just. Those who sold it to me
murdered them who lived on it before. I will manage it myself, as
your steward, my brother will assist us, we shall live happy, like the
family of the Shariers in the parish of St. Mary's, who have all things
common. The Christians of old, attempted this happy mode of
living in fellowship or brotherhood, but, after the death of Christ
and the apostles, the national priests persuaded their emperor to
establish the Christian religion, and they also embraced, in hypocrisy, the Christian faith. They took possession of the Church
property. and called it theirs, which remains in their hands to this
day; but they have taken care to hedge it about with laws which
punish with death all those who dare attempt to take it away. Yea,
the bayonet is engaged to enforce the law, should the people
discover the trick, and prove turbulent; and the Clergy, for this
military security, pervert the doctrines of Christ, which ordered the
sword to be put up, it not becoming his followers to shed human
blood. The clergy practically declare, that Christ knew not what he
said; they being wiser than him persuade the people to draw the
sword, contrary to the command of Christ, and slay their brethren.
They threatened with eternal damnation all who dare refuse obedience to their command; but they are very kind to persuade you to
confess you are guilty, when you are not, but Cashman[3], Bellingham, Despard, and the political sacrifices in France, were not to be
cozened by hypocrites, the holy league with the Pope will not be
able to hoodwink the people, though Lewis the 18th is labouring
hard, priescraft cannot be grafted on the philosophic tree of liberty.
You see Miss Campbell, the necessity of the exortation I give your

people, watch your priests, pay them for their labour, never let them meddle with your worldly affairs.

To be continued

THE SLAVES

An Elegy

IF late I paus'd upon the twilight plain
Of Fountenoy, to weep the free-born brave.
Sure Fancy now may cross the western main[4],
And melt in sadder pity for the slave.

Lo! where to yon plantations drooping goes,
The sable herd of human kind, while near
Stalks a proud despot, and around him throws
The scourge that wakes—that punishes the tear.

O'er the far beach the mournful murmurs run,
And join the rude yell of the tumbling tide,
And faint they ply their labours in the Sun,
To feed the luxury of British pride.

E'en at this moment, on the burning gale
Floats the weak wailing of the female tongue;
And can that sex's softness nought avail—
Must naked woman shriek amid the throng?

Oh cease to think, my soul! what thousands die
By suicide, and toil's extreme despair;
Thousands, who never rais'd to heaven the eye,
Thousands who fear'd no punishment but there.

The drops of blood, the horrible manure
That fills with luscious juice the teeming can
And must our fellow-creature thus endure,
For traffic vile, th' indignity of pain?

Yes, their keen sorrows are the sweets we blend
With the green bev'ridge of our morning meal,
The while we love, mock mercy we pretend,
Or for fictitious ills pretend to feel.

Yes, 'tis their anguish mantles in the bowl,
Their sighs excite the Briton's drunken joy;
Those ign'rant suff'rers know not of a soul,
That we enlighten'd may its hopes destroy.

And there are men, who, leaning on the laws.
What they have purchas'd, claim a right to hold—
Curs'd be the tenure, curs'd its cruel cause—
Freedom's a dearer property than gold!

And there are men, with shameless front have said
That nature form'd the negro for disgrace;
That on their limbs subjection is display'd—
The doom of slav'ry stampt upon their face.

Send your stern gaze from Lapland to the Line,
And ev'ry region's natives fairly scan,
Their forms, their force, their faculties combine,
And own the vast variety of man!

Then why suppose yourselves the chosen few,
To deal oppression's poison'd arrows round,
To gall with iron bonds the weaker crew.
Enforce the labour, and inflict the wound?

'Tis sordid int'rest guides you; bent on gain
In profit only, can you reason find;
And pleasure too but urge no more in vain,
The selfish subject to the social mind.

Ah! now can he, whose daily lot is grief,
Whose mind is vilified beneath the rod,
Suppose his Maker has for him relief?
Can he believe the tongue that speaks of God?

For when he sees the female of his heart,
And his lov'd daughters torn by lust away,
His sons, the poor inheritors of smart—
Had he religion, think ye could he pray?

Alas! he steals him from the loathsome shed,
What time moist midnight blows her venom'd breath,
And musing how long he has toil'd and bled,
Drinks the dire balsam of consoling death!

Haste, haste, ye winds, on swiftest pinions fly,
Fre from this World of misery he go,
Tell him, his wrongs bedew a nation's eye,
Tell him Britannia blushes for his woe!

Say, that in future, negros shall be blest,
Rank'd e'en as men, and man's just right enjoy;
Be neither sold, nor purchas'd, nor oppress'd,
No griefs shall wither, and no stripes destroy!

Say, that fair Freedom bends her holy flight
To cheer the infant, and console the sire;
So shall he. wond'ring, prove at last delight,
And, in a throb of ecstacy expire.

Then shall proud Albion's crown, where laurels twine,
Torn from the bosom of the raging sea,
Bend 'midst the glorious leaves, a gem divine,
The radiant gem of pure humanity,

DELLA CRUSCA

NOTES

1. Miss Campbell. Robert Wedderburn records that his mother
    Rosanna was eventually purchased by the Campbell family in
    Kingston, who treated her kindly, unlike his own father and
    her other owners. Miss Campbell appears to have been the
    heir to the sugar estates and may have been a mulatto.
    Wedderburn implies that she possessed Maroon ancestry and
    that she was his sister—they could have shared the same
    mother, Rosanna. The correspondence published here may
    be fictitious but Miss Campbell herself was probably real
    enough.
2. John Palmer (1742?–1798), a celebrated though impoverished
    actor who is said to have had French Revolutionary sym-
    pathies. Wedderburn is referring to his spectacular death
    which occurred onstage in the third act of a performance of
    'The Stranger' on 2 August 1798.
3. Cashman was an Irish fisherman and sailor with a long and
    heroic record of service in the Napoleonic wars, who had
    been discharged without receiving owed backpay and prize
    money. During a drunken spree, he joined the Spa Fields riot
    of 2 December 1816, unaware of its Spencean and ultra-
    radical connections. His capture and execution aroused im-
    mense popular animosity in London. John Bellingham also
    nursed a grievance for money owed to him by the government

for a Russian business transaction; he became so incensed that he shot and killed the Prime Minister, Spencer Perceval, in the House of Commons on 11 May 1812. Though transparently insane, he was executed at Newgate. Such was the government's unpopularity that he became something of a folk hero. So too—with greater justification—did Colonel Edward Marcus Despard (1751–1803). Of Irish extraction, with an illustrious military career which included distinguished service under Nelson, he too was shabbily treated by the government who failed to pay him substantial owed compensation and then imprisoned him in 1798 for his persistent complaints. Thereafter, he became closely associated with disaffected Irish emigres in London, as well as the United Irish and United English revolutionary underground. He was in the process of planning armed uprisings in England and Ireland when he was seized by the government in a Lambeth tavern in November 1802. Despite a strong plea in his defence by Lord Nelson, Despard was found guilty of high treason and executed on 21 Feb. 1803.

4.　'The Atlantic Hesperian Mare, so called by the antients.'

No. 5.   *Price Threehalf-Pence.*

THE

AXE LAID TO THE ROOT,

OR A

FATAL BLOW TO OPPRESSORS,

Printed by A. Seale, 160, Tottenham Court Road; and Published by
Robert Wedderbur[n] 8, Church Lane, St. Martin's Lane, London.

Continued from No. 4

Lest any one should accuse me of having a secret enmity against
the Clergy, I will here explain why I warn my countrymen to be
on their guard. First, the apostle directed the Church, in his day,
that the preachers of the gospel should administer in spiritual
things, deacons were appointed to administer in temporal, so
that any clergyman who meddles with worldly affairs, must, of
necessity, neglect the spiritual concerns of the church; besides,
the laws of England will not suffer a clergyman to be a member
of the House of Commons; and those who act as magistrates,
discover a great degree of tyranny and ignorance in worldly
matters: the people, through respect, are bashful, and will not
reprove them, for errors committed in worldly affairs, so they
continue in their ignorance till they become vicious, and commit
crimes which I am ashamed to record. This may be traced up to
the head of the church, whether Protestant or Popish.

R. WEDDERBURN.

7

The Axe Laid to the Root No. 6 [1817]

FROM MISS CAMPBELL TO ROBERT WEDDERBURN,
THE SPENCEAN

DEAR BROTHER,

By setting my slaves free, and giving them the land, agreeable to Spence's plan, it has cast me into a gulph of trouble, for, when I went to have the deed recorded, the governor's secretary made a long pause, then told me he never heard of such a doctrine, he was not furnished with any legal form in which he could enter my will; he told me it was necessary the governor should be acquainted with it; I was then brought before him, he looked at me with a pleasing steadiness and said, My Dear, have you taken leave of your senses, to set your slaves free, and give them the land, such an idea never entered the mind of any one that ever existed who held the land as private property, and human beings as slaves, therefore you must be in a state of delusion. Oh! no Sir, I am not, I was told to do it by my brother, and since I have done it I have felt my heart enlarged to love the whole human race. I can now keep the first and second commandments with joy; yes, I now, indeed, love my neighbours as myself. Hold your tongue, Miss Campbell, you have been listening to the Methodists. I say, God bless the Methodists, they teach us to read the bible, and there it is written, that the slave which would not accept his liberty at the end of the seven years jubilee, must have his ears cut off, because he loved his master and mistress, and despised the law of liberty; he was never to have the benefit of another jubilee while he lived, Why, you have turned preacher, Miss Campbell; where is your licence? Why, Sir, Jesus Christ and the apostles, had their licence from God. I think it is a crime, Sir, to ask a licence of any man to speak the truth even at the risk of my life, as a Christian. Well, child, I will hear you on this head at a more

105

convenient time, but, in the mean while, keep your slaves upon your own estate, for fear they should corrupt others, and turn their brains to think that liberty and possession of the soil is better than slavery and the whip. There is a law made by the assembly, to hang a slave. One has been hung for preaching, teaching or exhorting, another has been hung for throwing up his hoe and blessing the name of King George, through mistaking the abolition of the slave trade for the abolition of slavery. Your people, whom you have foolishly set free, are liable to the law till their freedom is recorded and then there is a fine of twenty pounds for each slave to whom they preached, for which they will be imprisoned, for the judges and juries and the assembly that make the laws, are all slaveholders. It is a pity but you could wait fifteen or twenty years longer, for there will not be a white man on the island then. But, Sir, the deed is done, I will obey you and keep them on our estate, but they have been talking about it this month past to the country negroes on the market days. I told them not to speak of it, but they talked of it the more. The news is gone to Old Arbore and St. Anns, to the Blue Mountains, to North Side, and the plantain boats have carried the news to Port Morant, and Morant Bay. I hope, Sir, they will not suffer for what they did in ignorance: indeed had they attempted to keep it a secret, the oysters would have jumped off the trees.[1] He bid me then to hold my foolish tongue, and go home, I curtsied and thanked him, and as I was going out, heard him muttering, there will be more white blood spilt in Jamaica than was in St. Domingo. I have been told since by a young gentleman, that the governor had got the newspaper from England, which gives an account of the Spencean doctrine. I could not believe him, then he pulled out a newspaper from his pocket and read it to me.

I was quite surprised to find that the good people of England were so much against the Spenceans: I thought the Blacks were the only objects of slavery and oppression. It is true what Solomon said, the rich hates the poor, no matter what colour. You will send me word what Sir Frances Burdett thinks of it. The newspapers say he is a very good man. I have been reading about Coke, of Norfolk, when at a public meeting, he confessed his ignorance of the Spencean doctrine. How is it a man can be ignorant, who has been a Member of Parliament for forty years, and holds a great deal of land as private property, receives a great deal of interest money, which is the same as wages from slaves, with this difference—a slave has a house for nothing, and pays no wages when he is sick. I, who am a weak woman, of the Marroon tribe, understood the Spencean doctrine directly: I heard of it, and obey, and the slaves felt the force directly. They are singing all day at work about Thomas Spence, and the two Evans' in Horsemonger Lane prison, and about you too, brother, and every time they say their prayers, they mention the Evans', they say that God Almighty will send the angels in his time, and let them out, in answer to our prayers. I believe, through the weakness of the Prince Regent, and the wickedness of Castlereagh, and Sidmouth, who imprison without crimes, and let them out without trial after running them and their families, without remuneration, has been the cause of God Almighty smiting the Princess Charlotte and the babe I think so, because the first born of Egypt were slain; they oppressed the poor people till they were afraid of rebellion, then they committed injustice, and punished the innocent to keep the starving poor quiet, adding sin to sin, till they filled up the measurs of their iniquity. Then God Almighty will set fire to them, and burn up the wicked, both rich and poor; for the poor who side with the rich, as the instruments of oppression will be destroyed: the poor that composed Pharoah's army were all drowned in the red sea. Had they turned round and shot their officers then fallen down on their knees, prayed to the God of Israel, Moses would have said to them, as he did to Gethro, come along with us, and we will do thee good, for the Lord has spoken good concerning Israel. Moses would not have called them murderers, for he himself had killed an Egyptian, knowing it to be the will of God. That the slaveholders and oppressors ought to be slain, these soldiers might have had plenty of sweathearts in the land of Canaan, after slaying all but the virgins. No doubt they would have had a share of the lands, for good soldiers have always something given. Witness the Duke of Bedford's family, and the offers now made in South America; but, according to Spence's plan, they and their families would possess their share of the rents for ever and ever, without swallowing up the property of others, as the Duke of Bedford's family and the like are now doing, thro' the system of private property in lands. Agreeable to what you mentioned in your last letter to me, there are a great many English officers who have come over here since the war, to be negro drivers, they are not so reserved as the Scotchmen, so that their black girls know a great deal more than they ought; they tell all they hear, to others; it is a common thing to hear the officers damn the planters, because they sell the poor white men's children, if the mother be a slave: the Scotch negro drivers never care about their children being slaves; you know what your father did.

The free Mulattoes are reading Cobbett's Register, and talking about St. Domingo: a great many of the Spaniards fled here, you must know, and brought their favourite slaves with them from St. Domingo, and the young men of Jamaica go amongst them, so they know the cause of their masters' coming to Jamaica. The slaves begin to talk that if their masters were Christians they would not hold them in slavery any longer than seven years, for that is the extent of the law of Moses. The planters' look frightened the slaves know what it is about, they dare not speak, nor smile, for they would be hung for suspected conspiracy. The governor has ordered the assembly to meet directly to see what is to be done, but my sweetheart, who is a very sensible young man says, they can do nothing, for the leven is laid too long in the dough, and and as the slaves are their bread, they must not hang them all. I shall, if God spares my life, send you all the particulars respecting the assembly, and the state of the island in general, in my next letter.

I send this letter by a black cook: I dare not trust it to the Post, for they open people's letters.

I remain

      Your affectionate

        Sister,

           Campbell

FROM MISS CAMPBELL TO R. WEDDERBURN

DEAR BROTHER,

In my last letter I mentioned that the governor had ordered a meeting of the assembly, chiefly to take into consideration the state of the island in general the meeting took place, the particulars were not suffered to be published, fearing it should fall into the hand of the slaves, for many of them can read and understand, and were it not for the young man who keeps my company, I should not have been able to give any information of the proceedings. He informed me that when the governor laid my case before them, not one of their orators attempted to speak for some time. The governor then asked, why was this silence, gentlemen, the business is serious, and you are all interested in it. One Mr. Macpherson replied, that he heard of Miss Campbell practising the Spencean doctrine, and he had made up his mind upon the subject, which was, that such slaves and lands set free by any Spencean enthusiast should not be entered on the records, and to check other owners from the like attempt, Miss Campbell should be considered as a lunatic, and be treated as such; for, if this assembly was to countenance such a degree of madness, as to tolerate, by law, any individual giving liberty to their slaves, and a right to the soil, we should then become actual Spenceans.

Gentlemen, it would be as imprudent as allowing a man to set fire to his own house, in a city. Are we not all in jeopardy? It is your duty to act as the British Senators have done: suspend all laws, imprison the Spenceans, as madmen, and let the proprietors of the country arm themselves, agreeable to the assertion of Sir Francis Burdett. I would advise the House to send immediately to England for a million of gags, one million yards of chain, one million iron collars, and to send to Scotland for one hundred thousand starving Scotchmen to manage the slaves, and I recommend to this honourable assembly to petition my Lord Castlereagh to command the Prince to order them to withhold licence from all dissenting preachers, the Wesleans in particular, and to call back to England all those that are in the island, for it is in vain for you to inflict death on the slaves for preaching, or exhorting their fellow slaves to embrace various new doctrines, which are calculated to impress the minds of the slaves with a desire of liberty, which is a direct violation of the laws of England, which authorise us to hold the Africans and their offspring as private property; and, unless our petition is attended to, I will recommend a revolt; there is no danger to be apprehended from any European power, for their strength is scarcely sufficient to keep their starving subjects in obedience to their will. Gentlemen, it is time you should begin to act for your own safety, I have to inform this assembly, that I am in possession of a tract called the Axe Laid to the Root, or a Fatal Blow to Oppressors, addressed to the Planters and Negroes of this Island. The tract is written by a native of this island, now in London, he has found means to convey them here; the effect has been the cause of this meeting, to take into consideration the recording of the freedom and surrender of lands through the delusion of Spenceanism, which, I oppose, with all my soul, and earnestly solicit this House will decree, agreeable to the assertion of many able lawyers of the British House of Commons, that the Spenceans are madmen, and ought to be treated as lunaticks; therefore, I move, that Miss Campbell be taken charge of as such, and her slaves and land be taken care of by the government, and place Mr. Cruckshanks, the Negro-driver, for their overseer, and place a church parson over them, to eradicate, if possible, the Spencean delusion from their minds, and the false notion that freedom is better than slavery or the whip: I would also recommend that a reward be offered for the Axe Laid to the Root to be delivered up to the Secretary's office: if by a slave, he shall be made free, on condition he will never preach the doctrine of Spence, but give information of all such slaves as are in possession of any of the writings of the Spenceans: and if a free man, he should be rewarded with one of the finest slaves that the estate of a deluded Spencean will afford. I recommend to this assembly, to import from England, a sufficient number of servants, to attend your persons, as domestics, you may have them for their food: yea, they would engage to serve you for life on no better terms, for they are dying for want; they will strengthen your hands against the Blacks; it is dangerous to have slave servants about your persons, however faithful they may have been, it is not safe to trust them, for the wild notion of liberty, and an equal right to the soil; has a tendency to destroy that faithfulness and attachment towards us. They have superiors, who frequently rewarded them with the gift of their freedom. You will recollect, gentlemen, the slaves are not so ignorant as the Marroons were, when, after they had gained their own liberty, became instruments to guard the woods from being a harbour for other runaway slaves. You will also recollect, we have broken the treaty with the Marroons, by punishing one of their tribes without trial by their own judge and jury, for which they went against us, and were it not for the bloodhounds we got from Cuba, and their magazine being discovered, we do not know what would have been the consequence; besides, we transported the whole of that tribe into a cold climate, which destroyed the chief part of them. Now, gentle—

To be continued

[Periodical ceased publication at this point]

NOTE

1. The oysters grow on trees in Jamaica.

PART IV

Insurrectionary Preacher

Plate 3. Thistlewood's Plotters. 'Modern Reformers in Council—or—Patriots Regaling, engraved by I.R. Cruikshank, published by G. Humphrey, 3 July 1818.' (Courtesy of the British Museum)

8

Can it be Murder to KILL A TYRANT?

At Hopkins-Street Chapel,
Near *Berwick-Street, Soho*

On Monday Evening, August 9, 1819,

The Following Question will be DEBATED,

'*Has a Slave an inherent right to slay his Master,
who refuses him*

HIS LIBERTY?'

*The Offspring of an African Slave will
open the Question.*

Chair taken at half-past eight o'Clock. Admittance 6d.

The case of Mr. Carlisle after two evenings Discussion in the presence of a very respectable Assembly, was decided in his favor without a discenting voice, and a monument proposed to be erected to perpetuate his praise.

The following Question will next be debated, viz.

IS IS POSSIBLE FOR THE GOVERNMENT TO BE
EXTRICATED FROM THE ACCUMULATING PERILS
WITH WHICH IT IS DAILY SURROUNDING ITSELF?

*Debates in future will be held twice a week, viz,
Monday and Wednesday.*

**N.B. Lectures every Sunday morning at eleven,
afternoon at three.**

E. Thomas, Printer, 5 Denmark Court,

9

PRO HO 42/195, Hopkins Street chapel, [9 Aug. 1819]

Wedderbourne—rose—Government was necessitated to send men in arms to West Indies or Africa which produced commotion. They would emply blacks to go and steal females—they would put them in sacks and would be murdered if they made an alarm Vessels would be in readiness and they would fly off with them This was done by Parliament men—who done it for gain—the same as they employed them in their Cotton factories to make Slaves of them to become possessed of money to bring them into Parliament.

The best Slave would be punished without evidence under certain circumstances—In speaking of a Black man who was hung for the murder of a Tyrant, he said he entered the Scaffold with great confidence and his manner indicated that his conscience felt no more guilt than Bellingham's or Cashman's.

Before six months were over there would be (or he hoped there would be) slaughter in England for their Liberty. Death was as acceptable as Slavery, and if he was to die for his Liberty it would rouse those he left behind him to kill their masters to gain their Liberty. The Scripture was contradition in itself. Common sense and reason not Scripture ought to be their guide. He produced a Bible and read the 16th verse of the 21st Chapter of Exodus 'and he that stealeth a man and selleth or if he be found in his hand, he shall surely be put to Death.'

The Bible ought not even to be admitted as Evidence in a Court of Justice. The Enlightened Israelites, protected their poor—*Every King, Bishop, Priest and Potentate ought to be put to Death for not putting that law in force*, being according to Scripture and Ancient Law. In alluding to Christ he said that a thief would submit to the offended justice of his Country and on the scaffold would suffer the rope to be placed round his neck knowing that Justice should be satisfied—and why should Christ have acted contrary to any other criminal *The Prince Regent, according to the Scripture, said the*

Oath he had taken to administer Justice ought to be put to Death for not administering it to his people.

He ridiculed Scripture very much. He said he had been endeavouring to offend that they might ring it in the ears of Kings, princes, Lords and commons—He had written home to the Slaves to avoid slaying their masters untill he knew the sense of that meeting.

———————

The sense of the meeting was taken,—Question 'has a Slave an inherent right to slay his master who refuses him his Liberty.'

Nearly the whole of the persons in the room held up their hands in favour of the Question.

Mr W. then exclaimed, well Gentlemen I can *now write home and tell the Slaves to murder their Masters as soon as they please.*

Sd. J. Bryant

10

PRO HO 42/191, [Rev. Chetwode Eustace], [10 Aug. 1819]

Your Lordship

                                                        10th. Aug. 1819

My Lord,
Yesterday Evening I proceeded to Hopkins St. Chapel to hear the
question discussed whether it be right for the People of England to
assassinate their Rulers, for this my Lord, I conceive to be the real
purport of the question tho' proposed in other terms—I had some
difficulty to discover the place for it is apparently a ruinous loft
which you ascend by a step-ladder—the assemblage was perfectly
suitable to their place for both Oraters and Audience were with a
few execptions, persons of the very lowest description.

The Doctrines were certainly of the most dreadful nature, and
two persons particularly distinguished themselves by expressions
which appeared to me most violently *seditious* and *treasonable*—
One of those men who appeared to be the principal in their concern
is a Mulatto and announced himself as the Descendant of an African
Slave—After noticing the Insurrections of the Slaves in some of the
West India Islands he said they fought in some instances for twenty
years for 'Liberty'—and he then appealed to Britons who boasted
such superior feeling and principles, whether they were ready to
fight now but for a short time for their Liberties—He stated his
name to be Wedderburn and said he was author of a production
entitled 'The Axe Laid to the Root' or some such name—but the
other person I think went even a greater length. Indeed some of
their expressions appeared to have shock'd even the worst of their
hearers. His question was adjourned to tomorrow Evening as
Wedderburn said he had been with about *two* hundred persons to
whom he gave a promise that the subject should be resumed—but
he might have said this merely as an inducement to those present to

116

attend on the succeeding night—Your Lordship will perceive that these persons are of the most contemptible description—however I fear they are too successful in their efforts to corrupt the lower orders. From what I have observed of these fellows I would most humbly recommend that some proper persons may be sent to watch their proceedings, and that prompt measures may be adopted for making examples of Wedderburn & such desperate characters who so fearlessly violate the Laws and avow their object to be nothing short of the assassination of their Rulers & the overthrow of the Government.

> I have the honour to be
> with the highest respect
> My Lord,
> Your Lordship's most obedient
> Humble Servant
> [Excised]

P.S. Should it be your Lordship's wish at any time to see me, you will be pleased to have a note directed to the case of Mr Stockdale
Pall Mall

11

PRO TS 11/45/167, Rex vs Wedderburn, Deposition of Richard Dalton, 13 Oct. 1819

Deposition of Richard Dalton resident no 24 Tiverton Row near Blackman Street Southwark in the Parish of St Marys Newington in the County of Surrey taken this 13th day of October in the year of our Lord, 1819.

Deponent on his oath saith that on Monday Evening last the eleventh day of October about half an hour past nine o'clock he proceeded in Company with Joseph Wood to Hopkins Street near Broad Street Soho to hear a Debate to be held in Hopkins Street Chapel.

Deponent also saith that on his arriving at the entrance of the said Chapel he this Deponent received a Ticket of admission from a Woman who kept the Door of the said Chapel in return for a shilling paid her the said Ticket having the representation of a head printed thereon which this Deponent was informed by the said Woman would admit him to any Debate or at the Sunday Lectures at the said Chapel during the space of one month.

Deponent also saith he thereon ascended a flight of wooden steps where he found about 80 or 90 persons assembled in a long room or loft with a Chairman presiding at a Desk.

Deponent further on his oath saith that a person was then addressing the Chairman and Company who he was informed was Wedderburn the preacher.

Deponent also saith that the said person which he understood to be Wedderburn was then haranguing the Company to revenge the murders committed at Manchester on the 16th August declaring with a vehement voice that the Revolution had already began in blood there and that it must now also end in blood here.

Deponent further declares that Wedderburn made use of the following words 'That the Prince had lost the confidence and affection of his people but that he the Prince being supported by the

Army and surrounded by his vile Ministers nothing short of the peoples taking arms in their own defence could bring about a Reform and prevent the same bloody scene taking place at the next Smithfield meeting as had taken place at Manchester'; 'for his part old as he was he was learning his Exercise as a soldier and would be one if he fell in the Cause for he had rather die like Cashman if he could but have the satisfaction of plunging a dagger in the heart of a Tyrant.' he the said Wedderburn declaring that the next meeting on 1st November would be such a general Meeting throughout the Country as well as London that then only would be the time.

Deponent farther on his oath saith that the said Wedderburn then also addressed the meeting with the loudest voice possible in the following words 'Therefore all come armed or its of no use and be sure you bring plenty ammunition with you'.

Deponent further saith that the said Wedderburn said he was convinced that on the question of the Evenings Debate the Character of the Prince was the most dangerously situated of the two.

Dept. also saith that on the sd Wedderburn's ceasing to speak the Chairman then addressed the Company by reading from a Bill the Question of the Evening's Debate which was as follows

Which of the characters are most dangerously situated the Prince who has lost the confidence [and] affection of his people or the subject who has gained it.

Dept. fa[r]t[he]r saith that the said Chairman then put the Question by shew of hands after which he declared the Question was decided that the Prince was the most dangerously situated.

Richd. Dalton

Sworn before me at the Bow Street the 13th day of Oct. 1819
    R. Birnie

12

PRO TS 11/45/167, Rex vs Wedderburn

Examination of William Plush

The following is a Copy of the Examinations relative to Wedderburn's Speech on the 13th

'Wednesday Evening Oct 13. 1819 went to Hopkins Street Chapel accompanied by Matthew Matthewson

Question Proposed was Which of the two Parties are likely to be victorious, the Rich or the Poor in the event of Universal War

... The second Speaker, Wedderburn, commenced with telling the Audience that he should intrude on their patience a little while having a few words to offer on the subject as he believed such a Question had never entered the Head of Man since the Creation of Adam—but a circumstance had occurred that had led him to frame the Question himself—There were but two classes of people in England very Rich and very Poor how did this happen? Why the Land was held by about 400 Families alone who took special care it should never go out of their families for all the Marriages of their children were made for gain the first question asked was what landed property has he got what estates is he Heir to? but who gave them this Land? God gave the World to the Children of Men as their Inheritance and they had been fleeced out of it—But now was the time to possess themselves of it, the Lords or Devils or whatever you like to call them had gone to France to spend that money which had ought to support some of the starving Poor—they knew the state the Country was in—they saw the People were determined no longer to put up with it and as such they thought it prudent to get out of the way of it and as for the Prince Regent why Ministers had transported him upon the Water and gave him plenty of wine and

two or three Whores and the poor Fool was very well satisfied and
so he dont care a damn about the peoples' sufferings—and as for the
soldiers they were very well satisfied unless it was those from the
Northern Districts for they couldnt get a Furlough to see their
Friends, particularly about Manchester—No, no, they would see
too much—they would hear about their Fathers, their Mothers,
their Brothers, or their Sisters that had been murdered and cut to
pieces by Yeoman Cavalry—there is another evil, Soldiers after
having served seven years are by Mr Windham's Act entitled to a
Penny a day extra, now on purpose to cabbage the loaves and fishes
to themselves, for we dont know what they do with the public
Money, they discharge them, they can get no employ they become
dissatisfied and join us Jacobins—there was a fine young Man the
other day that I saw in a starving state, he had belonged to the Life
Guards and was discharged without a pension there was a pretty
reward for his services Oh! such a rotten Government—I took him
to a Jacobin House filled his Belly and brought him here last Sunday
and collected 4/6d for him—the fools dont think such Men as these
will assist us in our Cause—but what made the rest of the soldiers
satisfied why they got a ninepenny Loaf for 6d. Meat that we are
obliged to pay 10d or 11d a pound for they get for 6d and they can
get Furloughs, the others that I before alluded to can't so that
faction is divided but we can make them all of one mind for poor
ignorant Devils what do they know they are content provided they
can get their Bellies filled—how shall we accomplish that? why
there is that *powerful* engine the Press that has done more than all
the fighting and all their Meetings at Aux La Chapple put together
—suppose we were to buy a Press of our own and get a Jacobin
Printer to work it then I dare say we could get a Jacobin Bill Sticker
who would stick up our Placards at Night at the corners of the
Streets—then as I said before as the Soldier is satisfied with his
Ninepenny Loaf for sixpence and his pound of Meat at the same
rate we must promise him he shall have them for nothing then as
Plunder is the Soldiers trade we must promise him a weeks plunder
that would settle the faction I warrant you—that would do more
than all the achievements of Lord Wellington on the Continent—
the Press is our only recourse—although they may burn by the
hand of the common Hangman Mr Carlile's publications of Paine's
Age of Reason, Common Sense, and Rights of Man they cannot
burn it out of my Head for they may hang me I pretty well know

that Lord Sidmouth, Lord Castlereagh, Mr Vansittart and jumping fiddling monkey George Canning *will lose their Heads*—they tell us to be quiet like that *bloody spooney Jesus Christ* who like a *Bloody Fool* tells us when we get a slap on one side of the Face turn gently round and ask them to smack the other—But I like jolly old Peter give me a Rusty Sword for as they have declared War against the people and the Prince Regent has sanctioned it by his fine vote of thanks and has turned a deaf ear to our petitions we must redress our own grievances my motto is Assassinate stab in the dark Oh! the 16th of August was a glorious day the Blood that was spilt on that day has cemented our Union. Oh! Blood is a fine cement for Blood is thicker than water God be praised—But Gentlemen are we to be governed by the like of that ignorant insignificant smock faced stupid fool that fellow that cut his throat Whitbread proposed for Westminster—I mean Earl Percy for although Mr W. acted as Prompter he had not sense to follow—No—Glory be to Thomas Paine—his rights of Man have taught us better.

Wm. Plush 20 Red x St. Borough—

Matthew Matthewson

13

PRO TS 11/45/167

In The Kings Bench Sittings after Hilary Term Middlesex,
The King ag[ains]t Robert Wedderburn for Blasphemy,
Brief for the Crown

MICHAELMAS TERM 1819 . . . . INDICTMENT FOUND
AGAINST DEF[ENDAN]T

HILARY TERM 1820 . . . . DEFT PLEADED NOT GUILTY
COPY OF THE ISSUE IS HEREWITH LEFT

CASE

FOR some time past Debates of a very seditious and blasphemous nature have been held in a Room at Hopkins Street which is commonly called Hopkins Street Chapel Deft was a frequenter and a principal Leader in the debates. Persons were admitted by a ticket for which a small sum of Money was given. The Witnesses who will prove the Blasphemous words spoken by the Def[endan]t were sent to the Chapel for the purpose of hearing and reporting what should be said on this occasion.

Proofs

TO PROVE that on Monday night Oct 28th 1819 he went to Hopkins Street Chapel in company with Matthew Matthewson that the question proposed for discussion was.*whether the refusal of Judge Abbott to Mr Carlile's reading the Bible in his defence was to be attributed to a respect he had for the Scripture or a fear that the absurdities & falsehoods it contained should be exposed* that after two other Persons had spoken on the question Deft after paying some compliments to the preceding Speakers said that Christianity it was true had been introduced but had never been followed—that Judge Abbott no doubt had read the Bible and knew pretty well the absurdities it contained. Jesus Christ said no man had ever seen

God, then what a damned old liar Moses must have been for he tells us he could run about and see God in every Bush; Christ says no man ever conversed with God and yet Moses had a long conversation with him thus one or the other must be liars, then there was Balaam's Ass, oh yes that spoke, and yet they tell us God put the words into his Mouth; then I suppose God got into the Jack Ass—then there was the pretty story they tell us about the Witch of Endor—Saul who had been destroying all the Witches as Devils or what not at last sends for the Witch of Endor to raise up old Samuel to tell him what he was to do. Now Jesus Christ tells us that no one can raise the dead but God—then the Witch must have the power of God—then we are told by this same Book that the Souls of the departed either go to Heaven or Hell, then was Samuel walking about in the Matter that composes the earth or was he gone to Heaven or Hell. Suppose he was in the Earth, then no one according to Christ but God in that case could raise him. And yet we are told that the witch did raise him and if in Heaven what power could bring him down not the power of a Witch who according to their account was leagued with Devils and persecuted as such. OH!!! how unfortunate for them that the parsons or priests should leave this for us to find out! Jesus Christ by the New Testament taught the Christian Religion but as religion is a part or parcel of the Law of the Land (as our friend says) your fat gutted parsons priests or Bishops would see Jesus Christ damned or God Almighty either rather than give up their Twenty or Thirty thousand a year and become poor Curate's at Twenty pounds per Annum but what did he teach us what did he say Acknowledge no King (he was a Reformer) now every King is a Lord then he meant acknowledge no Lord, because every King is a Lord, every Person is the same that bears the name as he lords over us; but then he is the Lords anointed. Jesus Christ says acknowledge no Rabbi (no priest) no he knew their tricks and he says stand it no longer then Jesus Christ says acknowledge no Fathers, why? because Fathers at those days were allowed by Law to thresh their Sons at any age, the same is allowed in Russia even to the present day.

Times were bad then and Christ became a Radical Reformer. Now I never could find out where he got his knowledge but this much I know by the same Book that he was born of very poor parents, who like us felt with him the same as we now feel, and he says I'll turn. Mr Hunt and then when he had that exalted ride upon the Jack Ass to Jerusalem the people ran before him crying out *HUNT FOR EVER!!!* for that was one and the same as crying out Hosanna to the son of David—for as the Book tells us God told David there should never be one of the Family wanted to sit on the Throne of Israel till time should be no more, but who heard this beside David? No one—and yet Jesus Christ says no man ever conversed with God; why then his Grandfather David must be a liar—but Christianity consists only of what I told you before. Acknowledge no King—Acknowledge no priest. Acknowledge no Father. And this Gentlemen never was practised. For that stupid Fellow Paul his Apostle, that he left behind him, taught quite a different thing and He says pay your tribute Money pay Caesar, but why did he say this? Why because he knew his Master had lost his life for saying otherwise. So thought Paul I'll tell them to pay their Taxes, and then I may go and preach where I like, without being afraid of Spies such as Oliver or Reynolds or such as perhaps are now in this Room for Jesus Christ was betrayed by a Spy, he came out and says you must not let these people cry out Hosanna but he was so proud of his ride he thought he was going to be King of Jerusalem directly and he says I must not stop them for if I do the very stones will cry out. So at last came Mr Oliver or Mr Reynolds and gave him up to Pilate. Thus you see Gentlemen there never was such a thing as Christianity ever practised in the world how unfortunate for them that after having selected four Books out of four and thirty, they should leave so many absurdities for us to find out, and Judge abbott knowing them as well as us, thought it would not do have them exposed.

To confirm the Account given by the last witness—call Matthew Matthewson.

14

PRO HO 42/196, Richard Dalton, 'Wesleyan Methodists—Hopkins Street Chapel', 10 Nov. 1819

The following question was debated at Hokins Street Chapel
Wed. evening Novr 10th 1819

which is the greater crime, for the wesleyan Missionaries to preach up passive obedience to the poor Black Slaves in the west Indies, or, to extort from them at the rate of 18, 0–0–0 per annum, under pretence of supporting the gospel,

as soon as the question was given out Wedderburn came forward and addressed himself to the chairman and the two West Indian Blacks which where invited for last night by Wedderburn and that they might expose the villiany of our church and State by Sending out those vipers of Church Missionaries to suck the blood of the poor innocent Blacks in the West Indies and to make them believe the great God was with them but instead of God it was the devil and the Missionaries that was sent from London by the Secretary of State for the Home department and for no other motives than to extort money for by the great Wesleyans pretending to preach the Gospel to poor devils and passive obedience to the planters there masters, and these villians as he terms them are not a bit better than a theif that robs for his bread he is owan(?) to them, he moreover contends and will he says swear to the present day that in consequence of these Government missionaries or rather church robbers that if these poor black devils as he terms them if they have not got any money to give these Government Missionaries they are tied up and flogd and most unmercifuley indeed. Every Monday both blacks and whites and there children as well as themselves and who is this owing to why to the great heads of this Nation who are robing the poor. Every day by loading them with heavy burthens such as taxation extravagance and luxury as he says. we experience more and more every day but we must put a stop to them and have a free set in their places and then there will be some good done and not till then the day is fast approaching when they will see there error and be sorry for what they have done, the corn bill he observed was great blow and aimd at the poor peoples Guts only and to support the Church and State and the great Land owners— what did they care as long as they got there rents of there Tennants—the poor he contended might go to hell for what they cared as long as they [took] the money out of the pockets—whose pockets could it come from but such as ourselves we have I am sorry to say stood too long, is not the great head of all ashamed of himself if he is not he ought to be, to be led by the nose of his Ministers so long as he as been if he as not found them out he ought to be made to find them out the country as stood it too long Mr Carlile he says as opened the eyes of the whole of the united kingdom of Gt Britain they are awoke to the villiany that is in practice every hour and every day God send us better days we cannot have worse but God I think as nothing to do with us he too as forsaken us altogether Mr Carlile I think is pretty right and all they know it well—there was present last night two or three fresh persons I had not seen there before one particularly annoyd the great Mr Wedderburn and his two blacks by opposing him in the question first set on foot by Wedderburn whose language almost shook [the] room by his exclaiming against the Church Clergy there Missionaries send abroad—it all meant and that there aim was nothing else the questions did not come to a close on account of the time not allowing of it it broke up a little before 11 o clock and adjournd until Monday next Novr 15th.

Sir your very Humbl Servt

Richd. Dalton

15

PRO HO 42/199, fo. 134, John Davis, 21 Nov. 1819

SUNDAY 21ST NOVR. 1819

John Davis one of the Patrole says that

About 8 o Clock this morning on the side of Primrose Hill towards West End Hampstead, several men mustered and began marching and wheeling in a military manner in close order and open order, they divided into two Parties—8 in each party besides the man that gave the command, did not see any armed but each had a stick, which they shouldered and carried like a musket, they remained until a quarter past 10 when they separated, part went to Marylebone New Church and part towards the Jews Harp House —one of them a man of colour was very active he was on the right of one of the Divisions, three or four others who appeared to belong to them said they should not fall in this morning and went away—one of them then said they expected to muster a great deal stronger but they supposed it was too cold—3 or 4 had aprons on—John Smith another Patrole saw them at a distance—They would have followed but were apprehensive of being known.

PART V

Infidel

16

THE

ADDRESS

OF THE

REV. R. WEDDERBURN,

*To the Court of King's Bench at Westminster, on appearing
to receive Judgment*

FOR BLASPHEMY,

WHEN HE WAS SENTENCED TO

TWO YEARS IMPRISONMENT

IN

DORCHESTER JAIL

On Tuesday the 9th of May, in Easter Term 1820.

EDITED BY

ERASMUS PERKINS.

'Man has a right to think all things, speak all things, and write all
things, but not to impose his opinions.'

Machiavelli.

'Fabulas et errores ab imperitis parentibus discimus; et quod est
gravius, ipsis studiis et disciplinis elaboramus.'

Minutius Felix.

LONDON:

PRINTED AND PUBLISHED BY T. DAVISON, 10, DUKE
STREET, SMITHFIELD.

Four-pence.

131

EASTER TERM 1820; TUESDAY THE 9TH OF MAY.
THE KING AGAINST ROBERT WEDDERBURN.

The Defendant having been found guilty of uttering a blasphemous libel at the sittings after Hilary Term, appeared pursuant to a notice he had received from the Solicitors to the Treasury, to receive judgment.

THE LORD CHIEF JUSTICE went through the notes he had taken on the Trial, recapitulating minutely the words of the libel as stated in the indictment, and as given in evidence by each of the witnesses William Plush and Matthew Matthewson.

The Defendant was then asked if he had any affidavits to put in, to which he replied in the negative, but said he had something to say to the court, and proceeded to state:–

That however long the counts of the indictment against him might be; and however strongly they had been sworn to, yet he did not think he had said so much, or at least in the manner precisely as stated by the evidence.

That in consequence of his being thrown into prison, his chapel was shut up and his congregation dispersed, which circumstances had prevented him from seeking from amongst them evidence to contradict or invalidate the testimony on the part of the Crown. As for himself his memory was extremely bad, and it was impossible for him to recollect all he might have said on the occasion. Every observation he made arose spontaneous on the spur of the moment; his sermons or speeches were never the result of previous contrivance, but he did certainly remember to have spoken upon the story of the Witch of Endor.

His impression on this subject arose from the circumstance of seeing his aged grandmother, a poor black slave in the island of Jamaica, several times most cruelly flogged by order of her master, a white man and a *christian*, for being a WITCH; now as he, when a child, had frequently picked her pocket of sixpences and shillings, he was well convinced she could not possess the qualities and powers attributed to witches, or she must have detected his petty depredations. When he came to be a Christian, and read the story of Saul and the Witch of Endor, with these impressions upon his mind, that witches must be bad people, he could never bring himself to believe that such characters could work miracles and raise the dead.

The Defendant was proceeding with similar illustrations to show the origin of his scepticism, respecting Balaam's ass speaking, but the court considered his language was of a nature which they could not tolerate.

He then said, it might save time and prevent him wounding the ears of the court, if the paper was read that he had in his pocket, which was in the nature of a motion in arrest of judgment. He then put in a brief, which was read by one of the officers of the court as follows.

May it please your Lordships. I am well aware that the gentlemen of the bar will smile, at what they will call the vanity and presumption of a humble individual like myself, in attempting to address the court on an occasion like the present. They are welcome to smile, but I will tell them that the most brilliant efforts which the ablest of them could make, were I capable of employing them, would, be equally as useless in *this place*, and on *this subject*, as what I am now going to offer.

However humble I may be as a member of society, and whatever efforts may be made to degrade me and render me contemptible in the eyes of the world, I have nevertheless the pride, and the ambition, to flatter myself, that even my simple exertions will one day or other be of no mean importance to the cause I am embarked in, which is that of *Religious Liberty* and the *Universal Right of Conscience*.

If we would obtain the privileges to which we are entitled, neither death nor dungeons must terrify us; we must keep in mind the example of Christ and his apostles, of Penn and the primitive Quakers, who all promulgated *what they considered* was true and beneficial to mankind, without the slightest regard to the evil consequences which such, their bold, independent, and disinterested conduct might bring down upon themselves. What was the result? Christianity in the first instance, and Quakerism in the second, were established by the very opposition that they met with.

VOLTAIRE has justly observed, that 'Martyrs are productive of proselytes;' and the history of every age proves the assertion. The execution of Jesus Christ, a mild and amiable man, between two abandoned characters, excited sympathy in the breasts of the people, and roused a spirit of enquiry as to what were the doctrines for which he was condemned.

The early Quakers were a stern and stubborn set of men, determined both to risk and to suffer persecution in the attainment of their object; and by this means they ultimately secured, and do still enjoy, greater religious liberties than any other sect without the pale of the state religion. Why then may not the numerous *Latitudinarians* of the present day hope, by zeal, industry, courage, and perseverance, to gain that toleration which is granted to others; or I should rather say, those rights to which by the law of nature they are entitled; for the very term *toleration* is a *delusion*; and as our GRAND PATRIARCH,[1] hath well said, 'It is not the *opposite* of INTOLERANCE, but only its *counterfeit*'; and a very shrewd and acute writer[2] of modern times has remarked, that 'The legislature might as well pass an act to tolerate and empower the Almighty to receive the worship of the Jew, the Turk &c. as to pretend to tolerate, or permit to suffer either of those characters to worship their respective gods according to their several and peculiar notions.'

I feel firmly persuaded, that no effort, however humble, will ultimately be lost to the cause of Truth and Liberty; and that even my trifling productions may, perhaps, 'Like bread cast on the waters, be seen after many days.' The progress of TRUTH is *slow*,' says HELVETIUS, 'and may be compared to a stone thrown into a lake; the waters separate at the point in contact, and produce a circle; that circle is surrounded by another, and that by others still larger, and so on, until they break against the shore, and become mingled with the general mass.' It is by these slow degrees that all new truths are propagated, because they must necessarily meet with considerable opposition from the ignorant, the prejudiced, and above all, *from those whose interests would be injured* by the public adoption of these new truths.

Having made these general observations, I shall now proceed to offer some reasons, why judgment should not pass against me; but I must only be considered as doing it in the character of an advocate for religious liberty, and not as one asking for mercy, or fearing, or wishing to avert your sentence, however severe.

In the first place, I most solemnly protest against the authority of this, or any other court upon earth, to interfere with matters of conscience, and contend that they are superior to the controul of any human tribunal. Both the advocate on the part of the crown, and the learned judge who presided during my trial, evaded the main question, by stating, that I was not prosecuted for entertaining this, or that opinion; but for grossly reviling the religion established by law.

With all due deference to such high authorities, I humbly submit, that this is a sophism which will not stand the test of fair
examination; because, of what use is the liberty of thinking, or the
liberty of conscience, if we are not permitted to give vent to them.
The celebrated politician MACHIAVELLI, has said, 'Man has a right to
think all things, speak all things, and write all things, but not to
impose his opinions.' We have not however, to thank any human
being, for acknowledging our right to think; as 'tis neither in their
power, nor our own, to controul our thoughts; neither chains, nor
dungeons, nor the terrors of being burnt alive, can prevent us from
thinking freely; neither ought they to prevent us from speaking
freely, writing freely, and publishing freely; if we think we can
benefit mankind, by exposing falsehood and error.

JUSTIN MARTYR, one of the earliest and most learned writers of the
eastern church, being at Rome during the reign of Antoninus Pius,
and finding that the Christians were grievously persecuted in some
of the distant provinces, addressed two apologies to that emperor in
their behalf, pointing out in a very able manner the impropriety and
absurdity of religious persecution. In his second Apology he says,
'Reason informs, and admonishes us, that true philosophers, and
men of virtue, have in every age loved and honored the simple
Truth, and have turned aside from following the ancients, whenever
their opinions have been found erroneous and bad; and that the
inquisitive searcher after truth should prefer it to his life, and should
not be deterred by the fear of death, or the threats of torture, from
speaking and acting according to justice.'

In consequence of these apologies, that *Pagan* emperor wrote
to the states of Asia, not only forbidding the Christians to be
persecuted, but enjoining, that 'If any one hereafter shall go on to
inform against this sort of men, *purely* because they are Christians,
let the persons accused be discharged, although they are Christians,
and let the informer himself undergo the punishment.'

It is of no use, my lords, to say we are tolerated to worship that
power, or those *powers*, which the greater portion of mankind agree
in *placing* above NATURE, if we are to be checked at every moment,
and told we must not do it in this, or that manner; because
instruction by preaching forms a part of most religious worship;
and it must certainly happen, that when we are all assembled to
worship our common Father, we shall be found mutually abusing
each other, or, at least, the doctrines of each other.

How can the different priests, or teachers, warn their respective audiences against what *they concieve* to be erroneous, without endeavoring to place that error in the strongest light—to show that it is ridiculous—or absurd—or contradictory—or gross falsehood. Must not the Catholic enlarge upon the heresy of the Protestant; the Protestant upon the idolatry and superstition of the Catholic; the Dissenter upon the lukewarmness and formality of the church of England; the Unitarian upon the droll hypothesis of the Trinity; the Deist upon what he conceives to be the absurdities and inconsistences contained in that book which all the former revere as a divine revelation; and lastly, must not the Atheist (who has the same right with the rest,) when lecturing on his system, necessarily treat the whole as fables and fiction?

How, I ask, can religious liberty exist, if this be not permitted? How could the teacher of Nazareth, and his zealous disciples, have preached upon the purity and simplicity of their monotheistic system, without contrasting it with the absurdities of polytheism? Was it possible to establish a Deistical religion, without proving that the fables of the Grecian and Roman gods, goddesses, and demigods were not only false, but puerile and ridiculous—and was not this *openly reviling that religion which was identified with, and the foundation of all the administration of justice* in those countries.[3]

Eusebius in his life of Constantine the Great, records the following direction given by that emperor: 'Let those that are in error, enjoy the same peace and tranquility as the faithful; and restoration of intercourse may go far to reclaim them to the right way. Let none molest another; but let every one act as his conscience dictates. Let those who have a true opinion of the Deity, believe that such only as regulate their lives by the rule of his laws, lead a holy and upright life; but let those who conform not thereto, erect temples, (if they will,) and consecrate groves to vanity. And let no man in any point, of which he is ever so clearly convinced, offend in any wise, or endanger another; but when a man has discovered a truth, let him therein benefit his neighbour if possible, otherwise pass him by. For a man voluntarily to strive after immortality, is one thing; it is another to be compelled thereto by fear of punishment.'

I cannot help adding one more instance of princely liberality, worthy the imitation of modern potentates. It is from the annals of our own country: when Pope Gregory the First sent the monk

Austin, and forty missionaries, to plant the gospel in Great Britain, that prince, *though an idolater*, went out to meet them with the greatest courtesy, sat in the open air to hear their leader preach; and after listening to them attentively, made the following handsome reply, which we have preserved by the venerable *Bede*. 'Your proposals are noble, your promises are inviting, but I cannot resolve upon quitting the religion of my ancestors for one that appears to me supported only by the testimony of persons who are entire strangers to me. However, since as I perceive you have taken a long journey, on purpose to impart to us what you deem most important and valuable, you shall not be sent away without some satisfaction. I will take care that you are treated civilly, and supplied with all things necessary and convenient; and if any of my subjects, convinced by what you shall say to them, desire to embrace your religion, I shall not be against it.'

I shall now proceed to a second ground of argument, why judgment should not pass against me. It has no personal reference to myself; viz. the weak and narrow policy which dictated this prosecution; because those doctrines which would have been confined to my obscure chapel—to my small congregation,—are now by the fostering aid of my prosecutors, published to the whole world. They themselves are the means of widely disseminating that which they pretend to condemn. They have effectually advertized the very thing which they dislike. By preventing me from preaching, they have compelled me to become an author. They have dragged me from obscurity into public notice; and since they have made me a member of the Republic of Letters, I beg leave to recommend to their attention a critical, historical, and admonitory letter, which I have just published, '*Addressed to the Right Reverend Father in God, his Grace the Lord Archbishop of Canterbury, on the alarming Progress of Infidelity; and the means which ought immediately to be resorted to, to check its frightful career.*'

Lord Shaftsbury says, 'It is a hard matter for a government to settle wit,' and the great Lord Chancellor Bacon observes, 'The punishment of wits serves to enhance their authority; and a forbidden writing is thought to be a certain spark or truth, that flies up in the face of them who seek to tread it out.' And I appeal to the experience of all men, whether they have not uniformly perused a condemned libel with greater eagerness, and consequently received a stronger impression from it, than they would have if it had not been prohibited. My prosecutors evince great ignorance of human nature, if they think they can tell the world of the existence of a singular doctrine, or a curious book, without at the same time creating in them a strong desire to become acquainted with it. They should keep in mind the *allegory* of our great grandmother Eve, and the tree of knowledge. She was forbidden to taste its fruit, *lest her eyes should be opened*, but her curiosity could not resist the temptation to disobey, though the punishment attached was so great. Will my prosecutors admit that they are suppressing my opinions from the *same motives*, and that their ends are thwarted in a *similar manner*. I know I shall be told again, that 'tis not my doctrines, but my language, for which I am prosecuted. This I contend is contemptible sophistry. If I am a low, vulgar man, and incapable of delivering my sentiments in an elegant and polished manner, am I to be condemned, when I find two pages in the Bible most palpably contradicting each other, for asserting that one of them must be A LIE?—for stating the history of the Witch of Endor to be an idle tale, and old woman's story:—and for attempting to divest the simple Deistical and Republican system of Jesus, of those gaudy appendages, those trumpery additions, with which craft and ignorance combined, have conspired to corrupt its native purity, its original simplicity. If this is not permitted, if any system is to be considered infallible, a bar is put to all human improvement. They must look up the human understanding, (that most glorious ornament wherewith NATURE hath vouchsafed to embellish her creature man,) in the trammels of superstition. They must tell mankind that all other sciences may be improved with credit, honor, and reward, but that no new lights must be thrown on the science of theology, under the penalty of dungeons and death.

Many obstacles are cast in the way of improvement in the science of government, but I may call the game laws,—the right of primogeniture, and several others,—'Relics of feudal barbarism'— 'unjust infringements of the law of nature;'—I may ridicule them and revile them, and you have no law to punish me; but if I comment upon what I conceive to be errors, inconsistencies, or contradictions in the Act of Parliament Religion, in a plain and intelligible manner, I am to be thrown into a prison.

That excellent writer GORDON, in a work called *Cato's Letters*, says, 'whoever would overturn the liberties of a nation, must begin by subverting the freedom of speech;' but I have no fear that the

REMAINING liberties of this country can be destroyed as long as there are people willing to suffer, and I am proud in reflecting that there are hundreds like myself, who aspire to the crown of martyrdom.

My Lords, some persons in my situation would endeavour to press upon your consideration the jury's recommendation to mercy, and the long imprisonment I experienced before I was bailed out to prepare for my defence. But it is by no means my wish to obtrude these circumstances on the notice of your Lordships, as I am so extremely poor that a prison will be a home to me; and as I am so far advanced in life I shall esteem it an honor to die immured in a Dungeon for advocating THE CAUSE OF TRUTH, OF RELIGIOUS LIBERTY, AND THE UNIVERSAL RIGHT OF CONSCIENCE.

ROBERT WEDDERBURN

THE SOLICITOR GENERAL briefly remarked, that the defendant had been recommended to mercy because the jury considered him to have erred through ignorance, and for want of parental care in his early years, but this could not be the case, if he was the author of that paper, which displayed considerable information. The Defendant likewise informs us, that we have compelled him to become an author, and made him a member of the Republic of Letters. He calls our attention to a letter he has just published, addressed to the Archbishop of Canterbury; how does this tally with his supposed ignorance, and incapability of writing? [He the defendant begged leave to state that it was true he could not write, but that he had caused his ideas to be committed to writing by another person]

At all events, continued the learned counsel, the defendant is a most dangerous character, because he certainly possesses considerable talents, and those too of a popular nature, and calculated to do much mischief amongst the class of people to whom he was in the habit of addressing himself. It must be recollected that his place of holding forth was a *licensed chapel*, and he himself a *licensed preacher* of the Unitarian persuasion. All these circumstances formed a protection for him, and he made use of it for the purpose of undermining and reviling the Religion of the Country.

He complains that this prosecution is the result of a persecuting spirit, of religious bigotry; but we can assure him it is not on the score of his opinions, however offensive, but for the open, scurrilous, gross, and violent manner in which he has attacked scandalised, and reviled, the Christian Religion. If he had but delivered his sentiments in a cautious, decent, and guarded manner, this prosecution would never have been instituted, but such language as his, addressed to the lower orders of the community, can never be tolerated.

MR JUSTICE BAILEY, in pronouncing the sentence of the court, addressed the defendant to the following effect:—

You have been convicted by a Jury of making use, in a certain discourse, of the blasphemous and profane words which have been detailed in the evidence already recapitulated—language calculated to distress the feelings of those who entertain a reverence for the sacred scriptures. It could not be tolerated, it did not show ignorance, but he was sorry to say a perverted and depraved talent.

The book you so impiously revile is of great antiquity, and contains not only the religion of this country, but of many others, and of all civilised and enlightened nations. Much of it is held in esteem both by Jews and Gentiles, the Jews themselves being a monument of its truth, and the part which they venerate is not inferior to the other. It has received the sanction of ages, it is the foundation of all courts of justice, and consequently, whenever it has received any violent attack, this court has always shown the offenders that it was a great crime, and punished them accordingly.

The Christian religion wants not the arm of man or of the law to support it, but it is nevertheless the duty of those who have to protect the public tranquility, to prevent all attempts to destroy it. Those who have leisure to investigate its internal evidence, cannot be injured by such doctrines as these, for I am convinced no one can be an infidel, who will examine it with candour and impartiality. It contains nothing but good will towards man, it is calculated to render him more humble, more submissive, and every way a better member of society, and of course to advance the happiness of mankind.

Those persons who have an opportunity of calmly examining it want no protection, but there are a vast many who have ears to hear, but not leisure to study and reflect, and it is for their protection that this prosecution is instituted.

This is a country, certainly of great freedom, but that freedom must not be suffered to launch into licentiousness. I regret, from the nature of what you offer, and the document put in, that the same disposition of hostility towards religion, which animated you when you committed the offence, still appears to influence your conduct.

When persons stand upon the floor of this court to answer for an offence, it is possible they may diminish the quantum of punishment, by proving that they have repented of their crime; but you still persist in justifying it, which is an aggravation of your offence. It is our duty then to remove you, at least for a time, from society, that you may be prevented doing it a further injury by the dissemination of your dangerous doctrines.

The Court do therefore sentence you to be imprisoned for two years in his majesty's jail at Dorchester, and at the expiration of that time, to enter into sureties, yourself in £50, and two other persons £25 each, for your good behaviour for three years more.

The End.

NOTES

1. The Philosopher of Ferney. Wedderburn is referring to Francois Marie Arouet de Voltaire (1694–1778), the most famous deist philosophe, sometimes known as the philosopher of Ferney where his country estate was located on the French-Swiss frontier.
2. Paine.
3. Vide the Trial—Judge Abbott's charge to the jury.

17

CAST-IRON
PARSONS,
OR
HINTS TO THE PUBLIC
AND THE
LEGISLATURE,
ON POLITICAL ECONOMY,

Clearly proving that the Clergy can be entirely dispensed with, without Injury to the Christian Religion, or the Established Church, and to the great Advantage of the State.

In a Letter addressed to the Rev. Erasmus Perkins, B.A.

BY THE

REV. R. WEDDERBURN, V.D.M.

Author of a Letter to the Jewish High Priest on the Political Schemes of Moses;   A Critical, Historical, and Admonitory Letter to His Grace the Archbishop of Canterbury, on the progress of Infidelity;   and now suffering Two Years Imprisonment in Dorchester Jail for Blasphemy,   &c. &c. &c. &c.

LONDON:

PRINTED & PUBLISHED BY THOMAS DAVISON,
10, DUKE STREET, SMITHFIELD.

THREEPENCE.

142

A LETTER, ETC.

State Prison, Dorchester, July 28th, 1820

MY DEAR FRIEND,

YOU will naturally suppose that my solitary hours are much occupied with my favourite *hobby*, THEOLOGY; but a subject has at times engaged my attention, which is equally connected with political economy as with religion. I have even had the vanity to think that my humble lucubrations may be of importance to my country at this awful crisis of general disaffection and financial distress. I have therefore, after the most mature deliberation, determined, (should you approve it) to submit my plan to the legislature and the public, without further delay; and trust that you will, in that case, get our esteemed friend Mr. DAVISON, to print it, and send a copy in the first place to all his Majesty's ministers, and then to the members of both houses of parliament, the Bishops excepted. Spare no expense in the accomplishment of this undertaking, for I am so sanguine of its adoption, and of being rewarded with a handsome remuneration for my patriotism and ingenuity, that a few pounds will be no object.

I have felt great satisfaction when reflecting on the wonderful progress of the Arts and Sciences within the last few years, and I have often thought that the great Sir William Temple was an enthusiastic bigot in his veneration of the ancients, when he gave them the preference over the moderns, even as to the knowledge of the sciences. What he says of their poets, their historians, and the elegance and purity of style to which the Grecian and Roman writers respectively arrived, is perfectly just; but sure it must be allowed as a natural consequence, that in the arts and sciences, each succeeding generation should continue to invent and improve upon its precursor. It is true that some few of their arts are lost, but is there, I would ask, in all the relics of antiquity, or in the surmises of a Montfaucon, a Lipsius, or a Winckleman, any traces of an invention like the Steam-Engine, or of the powers of machinery being directed to a thousandth part of the purposes to which we now so happily apply them. Reflect but a moment on the rapid strides which chemistry has made within the last fifty years,—look at our manufactures—consider the countless modifications of which we have rendered the article of Iron susceptible—how innumerable are the ways in which it administers to our wants.—In the shape of pipes it conducts the water and gas-light to our houses.—in that of bridges it enables us to pass over the widest rivers,—it forms the main supports and bonds of our dwellings.—it has paved our streets,—supplied rafters for our roofs; in one instance devoted to ornament,—in another to strength,—in a third combining both; and last of all it furnishes us with coffins when we drop into our eternal sleep. Scarcely a day passes but it is applied to some purpose not thought of before; and the object for which I am now about to introduce its service, will infinitely surpass every scheme, which the human intellect has hitherto developed.

Not wishing, however, to arrogate too much to myself, I will candidly relate the generation of my plan:—I will recur to the first impression my imagination received,—show the original association of ideas which caused its conception, and describe its progressive arrival at perfection up to this moment of its glorious birth.

Happening to pass the old church of St. Paul, *Shadwell*, in the county of Middlesex, when it was taking down, I asked the Churchwarden (who stood by) whether the intended structure was to be of wood or stone? 'Of neither,' he replied, 'but of CAST-IRON.' '*Would to God the Parson were of Cast-Iron too*,' exclaimed an old apple woman, who over heard our conversation. This pious ejaculation sunk deep into my mind; I have brooded over it for these five years: it was the germ—the very fountain head of my proposition; and had it not been for the devout aspirations of this poor apple woman, it is highly probable the world would never have been favoured with *this pretty little book*,[1] a copy of which I request you will present her, if alive, and still keeping a stall on that spot, as some acknowledgment for an idea upon which a projection is founded so pregnant with important results—upon which perhaps the fate of empires may depend—and which may cause a grateful posterity to vote me statues of brass, and enrol my name in the temple of Fame!—such great events, at times, from trivial causes spring.

I had read the '*Hints of a Barrister to the Public and the Legislature, on the Nature and Effects of Evangelical Preaching.*' I had been in the habit of contrasting the line of conduct pursued by the Dissenting preacher with that of the Minister of the Church of England. I compared the one to an old established shopkeeper, who had become *well tiled*, *warm*, *fat*, and *saucy*, who in fact cared very little whether his customers came or staid away. I compared the other to an up-start, a new-comer, who depended entirely upon his own industry, and the exertion of his talents in gaining customers, in rendering his shop attractive, in being assiduous to please, and inculcating an idea that his commodity was not only far superior, but the only genuine article, and that what the other dealt in was both stale and spurious. I found that the one by the dint of ex-temporaneous discourse, delivered with zeal and energy, and directed to the passions instead of the understanding, made a very powerful impression on his hearers. He was an experienced master of human nature—he could elevate or depress his audience at pleasure—he could play upon them as a skilful musician upon a well-toned instrument; and when once their feelings vibrated in concord with his doctrines, they became his fixed and certain customers—heirs to a *new birth-right*, *babes of grace*, and *Citizens Elect of the Heavenly Jerusalem*. But the other was content to read cold and dry discourses on morality, no better than might be culled from Cicero or Seneca, addressed to the understanding rather than the passions, and in such a dull, drowsy, inanimate, and monoto-nous tone, that he lulled the greater part of his congregation to sleep. When this performance was ended, and they rose to leave the Temple of the *State* Religion, no vestige of the Sermon could be traced in their manners; they talked of nothing but the weather, business, of family affairs; whereas the followers of the Methodist Preacher when quitting their Tabernacle, were heard to exclaim, Oh, the dear man! the charming man! the wonderful man!—Some with a solemn and sanctified gloom on their countenances, others with a glow of joy indicative of the spirit's communication that their sins were for ever washed away by the Blood of the Lamb, and their name written in the Book of Life!

Finding that the routine of duty required of the Clergy of the *legitimate* Church, was so completely mechanical, and that nothing was so much in vogue as the dispensing with human labour by the means of machinery, it struck me that it might one day be possible to substitute A CAST-IRON PARSON. I had seen the automaton chess-player, the automaton portrait-painter, the mechanical figure of a beautiful lady who played delightfully on the piano-dulce, the motions of whose body were peculiarly graceful, her eyes alternately directed to the keys of the instrument, and in respectful reverence to the audience, and whose transparent kerchief discovered the respiring action of her snowy bosom.

But[2] in all these astonishing productions of art, there was one grand *desideratum*, viz. the imitation of the human voice, which was not yet accomplished, and was the 'consummation devoutly to be wished.'

Though this last perfection of automatonism was necessary to the completion of my plan, yet I did not despair of its being sooner or later accomplished, consequently I continued to prepare it in my mind that it might be ready for execution the moment some happy mortal should succeed in imitating by art, the human voice. Judge then the rapturous ecstasy I experienced, on discovering in the *Literary Gazette, or Journal of the Arts, Sciences, and Belles Lettres*, which you sent me, dated the 3rd of June, 1820, the following most important intelligence:—

'A German Journal asserts that an artist of Cemberg, in Prussia, has constructed an automaton which imitates the human voice, and answers questions in German and Polish.'

Here, then, my fondest hopes were realised!—from this moment I determined to make my plan known to the world, as it was now perfectly practicable. Situated as I am, in solitary confinement, it would be a most fascinating pastime for me, had I the materials, and were allowed the tools necessary to make a model, but as that cannot be permitted, I must content myself with possessing the genius to invent, and leave the mechanical part to others. I would have you submit the plan to the 'Society for the Promotion of Arts, Manufactures, and Commerce,' in the Adelphi; they can add it to the list of premiums which they offer for any desirable improvement; and vote me a gold medal, and 100 guineas as the original projector, and offer a reward to the artist who shall construct the best model for carrying my ideas into execution. But in the first place, as you are a member of that Institution, I should wish you to feel the pulse of the different gentlemen who compose the Committee of Mechanics, and if you find them timid, squeamish, and too aristocratically inclined to forward so bold an undertaking, they shall not have the honor of cooperating in so laudable a design, but we will have it done at our own expense, and you must step over to Cemberg, in Prussia, and engage the artist before mentioned to come over and construct the musical part, which gives the speech, and we can easily remunerate ourselves in this wonderful land for

Raree-shows and Charlatanism, by exhibiting it for a shilling a head.

I shall now give a slight sketch of the operative part of my scheme, which is as follows:—That the legislature pass an act to annul all Tythes and Church Emoluments whatsoever, and decree that from and after a certain day (in the said act to be specified) that the order of persons called Clergy, or Priests, Deacons, Curates, Rectors, Vicars, &c. of the Establishment, be totally annihilated, suppressed, and abolished. That every parish shall, immediately after that time, purchase one of the *Cast-Iron Parsons*, and retain the person who officiates as Clerk, to perform all his present functions, and moreover to superintend, keep clean, and wind up the mechanical Cast-Iron Parson. That the said Clerk shall be provided, at the expense of the churchwardens, and under the direction of the magistrates, with a sufficient quantity of short sermons, such as are sold at RIVINGTONS, in St. Paul's Church-yard, neatly printed in separate copy-books, but done in the *script* type, to appear at a distance like manuscript. That the sermons for the common Sundays be not used more than three times in one year, and that a sufficient number be also purchased for Christmas-day, Easter, and all other regular festivals, rites, and ceremonies of the Church, with proper and suitable discourses for the annual fast, the anniversary of a benefit club, the death of a rich spinster, bachelor, widow, married man or married woman, in order that the usual fees and presents received on the latter occasions may still be taken by the churchwardens towards defraying the parish burdens. And whereas there is at present in some parishes a wooden construction similar to a watch-box, for the minister to be sheltered in from the rain while performing the burial service in the church-yard, it is therefore ordered, that the intended Cast-Iron Parson shall have wheels after the manner of the said watch-box, in order that he may be with the greater facility removed from the pulpit to the communion table, to the baptismal font, or to the church-yard to perform the burial service. That all the regular and reasonable fees heretofore received by the minister of the parish, shall henceforth be taken by the churchwardens and overseers of the poor for the time being, except for burying the dead, which is on all occasions to be free of expense, as the poor dead creatures cannot bury themselves, and as it is a melancholy circumstance to their friends; but marriages and christenings being for the most part jollifications, people will not begrudge a trifle to have them registered and manufactured according to law. That in cases of emergency, and where people cannot die comfortably without him, the said Cast-Iron Parson may be taken to their residences on the contingent extra expenses being paid. That the clerk of the parish be paid an extra salary of £20 per annum for his superintendance of the said automaton, and that he be punctual in regulating the machinery in such a manner that the ordinary service of the day be gone through in a regular manner, always recollecting that his voice is to be wound up to a higher key when the sermon is placed before him. And provided also, that should the inhabitants of any parish think it necessary to keep up the old custom of having the discourse delivered from a more elevated situation than the reading desk, that in such case it shall and may be lawful to erect a crane and pulley, whereby, with the aid of a rope round the neck of the said Cast-Iron Parson, he may speedily be hoisted and easily lowered into the pulpit.

The Advantages of the proposed Plan

Are threefold;—I. To religion. II. To society. III. To the state.— Our holy religion can no longer be brought into disgrace by the bad lives of the clergy, for the Cast-Iron Parson cannot enter into party spirit, and family dissensions, nor be guilty of adultery, fornication, drunkenness, or gambling. He cannot incur the hatred of his richer parishioners by his avaricious and griping manner in gathering his tithes, nor can he excite the contempt of the poor by his proud, morose, and supercilious deportment.

Is not the Rector frequently embroiled in quarrels and litigation with his parishioner? And can they derive the benefit they ought from the holy Gospel of God, when preached by a man whom they have reason to abhor—whom they may perhaps consider as a hypocrite, a knave, and an overbearing tyrant? Can they consider such a man a fit herald to proclaim the doctrines of the meek and lowly Jesus, or a proper successor of the humble fishermen, his disciples? Is it not palpable that religious instruction must come with greater efficacy from an immaculate being like the Cast-Iron Parson, totally divested of human passions, and all those 'frailties that flesh is heir to.' Will not the bulk of society be grateful to the government for relieving it of one of its burthens, so long and so justly complained of? And will not the state be benefited, by throwing back into the hands of the farmer and the landholder one-tenth of the produce of their land which was hitherto taken, not for the government, but for the clergy—will they not thereby be the better enabled to pay their assessed taxes for the support of the state? And is not this a most important consideration at a period when we can hardly keep our heads above water, and are threatened every moment either with bankruptcy or revolution? Will it not please the Dissenters, who now compose two-thirds of the population, to be freed from supporting a system of which they disapprove?

OBJECTIONS ANSWERED

It may be urged that the Cast-Iron Parson cannot be a very watchful shepherd over his flock—cannot visit the poor, the fatherless, and the widow, to administer consolation;—admitted;—but all this is now out of fashion, and not requisite, since the Dissenters have entirely engrossed these laborious offices to themselves. It will be found too, upon a fair calculation, that the Established Church will be freed from far greater discredit by the substitution of the automaton, than it could derive credit by continuing the drones, under a system which is but ill calculated to produce pious, zealous, and indefatigible labourers in the vineyard of Christ. If the projected machine cannot go about to do good, it is equally incapable of hunting, shooting, horse-racing, card playing, or frequenting balls, routs, and other profane and ungodly amusements.

It may be said that my plan deprives the government of considerable support by destroying the legitimate Clergy, who have ever been convenient tools in their hands where-with to keep the bulk of the people in subjection, by preaching up non-resistance, passive-obedience, the Right Divine of Kings, or any other doctrine which might suit their purpose. But it must be recollected, that I have given the neighbouring *magistrates* the superintendance of the sermons which are to be placed before the automaton, consequently he will become a more certain and uniform engine of the government than a live parson. There have been instances of stubborn, headstrong, and independent men getting into the church, and what has happened once may happen again; therefore as the times are getting worse, and arbitrary measures more necessary to keep the *'swinish multitude'* in order, care must be taken against such an occurrence, by adopting my Cast-Iron Parson, who will at the end of every discourse say, *'Fear God, honor the King, pay your Taxes,*

be humble and quiet that you may enter the kingdom of Heaven.'
The magistrates are sufficiently numerous, in conjunction with the
churchwardens and overseers of the poor to regulate all parish and
ecclesiastical matters, without the aid of bishops, deans, prebends,
or consistory courts, and therefore all the enormous revenues which
were required for their support, will no longer be drained from a
people already impoverished, in consequence of which the poor
devils will be grateful, and bear the remaining burdens with less
grumbling.

I shall be told that it is very inhuman to turn 20,000 clergymen
thus suddenly out of employ;—but of what weight is humanity in
the scale, when the good of the state depends upon it. Is not the
revenue falling off every year? Is not the welfare of the state of more
importance than any one class of society? Will not the retrenching
of £3,000,000 annually paid to the clergy enable us the better to pay
the government taxes? How many thousand labourers and artizans
have been starved in consequence of the introduction of machinery,
and dispensing with human labour; but are a few thousand souls
that cannot be missed in a redundant population, to be thought of,
when by this means the great capitalist has been able to sell his
goods cheap, and pay the king's taxes, which he could not otherwise
have done? The inviolability of legitimate monarchy, the dignity of
the crown, and the pomp and splendour of a court, must be kept up
at all events, as it is by these means alone that the blessings of *social
order* can be preserved, therefore no sacrifice ought to be deemed
too great, and the clergy as the most loyal body of men, should be
the first to fall into my views, particularly as I have proved that
neither the Christian Religion, the Established Church or the state,
can possibly be injured thereby, but on the contrary, all materially
benefited. I am no enemy to religion, or the church, or the
government, but a friend to the whole—staunch and loyal to the
back-bone. This is no wicked, ironical, sarcastic, Jesuitical libel,
aimed at the destruction of the church, as by law established, but
merely the suggestion of a slight improvement in one of the wheels
of the great state machine, for the benefit of the whole. In an awful
hour like the present, when jacobinism and infidelily are making
such rapid strides, it is the duty of every good man to exert those
talents which divine providence has given him, in suggesting any
idea that may possibly save us from the dreadful gulf of ruin which
stares us in the face; and may the Lord, in his infinite mercy grant

his blessing upon my humble endeavours, is the prayer of your Friend in the BONDS OF CHRISTIAN FAITH,

ROBERT WEDDERBURN.

P.S. In those foreign countries where their Kings are mere drones, sunk in dedauchery and licentiousness, troubling themselves with nothing but their own pleasures, and so completely absorbed in luxury and effeminacy that they leave the management of state affairs to the knaves and parasites by whom they are surrounded, signing every paper at random which the minister lays before them,—in such cases as these I think a CAST-IRON KING would answer every purpose, and be a very great saving. You should send this hint to Naples, it may perhaps be of some use abroad, now that revolutions are so prevalent.

It has likewise occurred to me that as there are about 300 Members of Parliament who uniformly vote with the ministers, but are incapable of saying more than *Aye* and *No*, who yet, nevertheless, expect sinecures, places, pensions, titles, and other good things for themselves and their dependents, it would be a great relief to the government to have their places occupied by CAST-IRON MEMBERS OF PARLIAMENT, who could be so constructed as to say *Aye* and *No* in the right place. This would be a wonderful saving, and the better enable us to reward men of talent who could support the ministers by their wisdom and eloquence.

R.W.

FINIS

Works lately Published by T. Davison.

The interesting TRIAL of the REV. R. WEDDERBURN, for Blasphemy, with his DEFENCE at full length. Price 6d.

Also his ADDRESS to the Court on receiving Judgment. Price 4d.

A LETTER to the JEWISH HIGH PRIEST on the Origin of the Scheme of a Messiah. By the REV R. WEDDERBURN. Price 6d.

A Critical, Historical. and Admonitory LETTER to the ARCHBISHOP of CANTERBURY, on the progress of Infidelity. By the REV. R. WEDDERBURN. Price 6d.

HINTS on the Texture of the MIND, and the Manufacture of CONSCIENCE. By the REV. ERASMUS PERKINS. Price 6d.

The RUINS of EMPIRES, and the LAW of NATURE. With Notes. By C.F. VOLNEY. Price 3s.

A SHORT WAY WITH THE DEIST; or SOUND REASONS FOR BEING A CHRISTIAN. Price 1d.

Preparing for Publication

HIGH-HEEL'D SHOES for DWARFS in HOLINESS.

A SHOVE for a HEAVY-BREECH'D CHRISTIAN.

CRUTCHES FOR THE LAME IN FAITH.

Mirabaud's System of Nature

Is now Publishing in Weekly Numbers, price Threepence each; or in Parts on Superfine hotpressed Paper at One Shilling each. The First Volume may be had in Extra Boards, price 7s.

Printed and Published by T. DAVISON, 10 Duke, Street, Smithfield.

NOTES

1. I think Dr. Wedderburn is guilty of a Cobbettism here. EDITOR.
2. I have likewise heard of a machine, or clock-work schoolmaster, to teach all the sciences, called the TECHNICATHOLIC-AUTOMATOPPANTOPPIDON.

18

The Lion, 21 March 1828

THE TITLE

'The *HOLY LITURGY*, or *DIVINE SERVICE*, upon the principles of *PURE CHRISTIAN DIABOLISM*, most strictly founded upon the Sacred Scriptures and the most approved tenets of the Grecian, Roman, German, Genevan, and English Churches, being an Universal and proper form of prayer for all Christians, excepting those only, who impiously reject the Scriptural doctrine of the personal existence of the *DEVIL*; prepared for the use of the congregation which assembles under the pastorship of the *REVEREND ROBERT WEDDERBURN*. By SPECIAL COMMAND, London, Printed at the University Press, by, &c. *Cum Privilegio.*

THE PREFACE

'Startle not, gentle Christian reader, at the name of *DIABOLICAL CHRISTIANS*; but carefully as thou valuest thine Eternal Salvation, examine the Scriptural principle of this new sect, and say, if they are not justified, by all that is held sacred, in Christian Revelation, and by the most seriously disposed Christians. It is not a profane hand, it is not the hand of the reviler, that passeth over this page: but the hand of a most sincere Christian. He might not be of thy sect; but, for his dissent from thee, he is not the less a Christian. He hath most studiously deduced, from the Sacred Scriptures and from the little less Sacred Writings of the most holy men of the general Christian Church, the best and most consistent Christian tenets that he can find, agreeably to his own disinterested judgment, or agreeably to that judgment which is deeply interested in the present and future happiness of self and all mankind.

'The *DIABOLICAL CHRISTIANS* hold the doctrine, that the *ALMIGHTY GOD* is so full of power and goodness—power to supply all our wants, and goodness to dispose him so to supply them—that they cannot perceive the propriety of addressing

153

troublesome, complaining, and ill-judged prayers to a divine Being, who is alike omnipotent, omnipresent, omniscient, and omnibenevolent. To offer this Deity a prayer is, at least, to doubt his goodness and his attention toward us. To presume, that the *MAJESTY OF HEAVEN* can be offended at our ignorance and our general imperfections, is, to presume, in derogation from his omniscience and general perfections. Far be this failing, this presumption, from us, who associate in public worship, upon the principles of *PURE CHRISTIAN DIABOLISM*.

'OUR PRAYERS SHALL BE ALL MOST PROPERLY ADDRESSED TO THE *MAJESTY OF HELL*, to the "*GOD OF THIS WORLD*," to that IMPERFECT, that OMNIMALEVOLENT, though POWERFUL BEING, *THE DEVIL*. This it is, that will justify our assumed appellation of *CHRISTIAN DIABOLISTS*.

'We feel our justification, in the circumstance, that the *GOD OF HEAVEN* is so much above our imperfections, as to be a Being not to be feared; while the *GOD OF HELL* and "*OF THIS WORLD*," partakes in part of our character and imperfections, and is, consequently, from his power superior to ours, a *Being to be feared, to be worshipped, to be cajoled with prayer;* and it may be, that the *MAJESTY OF HEAVEN* will make us weak mortals instrumental in the conversion of the *MAJESTY OF HELL*, from the errors of his ways; that conversion and restoration having been divinely predicted, as the necessary preliminary to the consummation of all earthly things!

'We have said enough, in the plainness and simplicity of our hearts, as a preface, to our form of prayer; and, with the strong hope of doing good, of bringing about "*glory to God, and peace and good will among men*," we leave each Christian reader to form an opinion of its merits. Our congregation will be open: we shall shrink from no examination, and we invite full observation, before any one presume to judge and condemn us.'